THE ART
of
ITINERANT TEACHING
for
TEACHERS OF THE DEAF
& HARD OF HEARING

D1637379

by
Mary Deane Smith

Butte Publications, Inc.
Hillsboro, Oregon

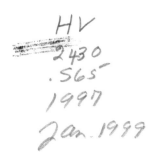

THE ART of ITINERANT TEACHING
for TEACHERS OF THE DEAF & HARD OF HEARING

Editor: Ellen Todras
Cover and Page Design: Anita Jones

Butte Publications, Inc.
P. O. Box 1328
Hillsboro, Oregon 97123-1328
U.S.A.

ISBN:1-884362-25-7
Printed in the U.S.A.

TABLE OF CONTENTS

ACKNOWLEDGMENTS

My thanks to Dr. Bill Brelje of Lewis and Clark College for urging me to write a book on itinerant teaching of the deaf and hard of hearing. Both Dr. Brelje and Dr. Laurene Gallimore of Western Oregon State College were most generous in their time and counsel.

Many staff members of the Columbia Regional Program for Deaf and Hard of Hearing have also been supportive, including Kristine Christensen, Donna Hodsdon, Cindy Kollofski, Julia Munson, Mona Todd, Larry Whitson, and the late Pam Pedersen. My thanks also to Marilyn Pardes of Alice Ott Middle School and Laura Rogers of Astor School, both in Portland, Oregon.

A special appreciation goes to the parents who contributed input for this book: Elaine and Earl Davis, Suzanne and James Holt, Marie Wolfe, and Pam Fussell. Some of my students also helped me with this project: Kevin Davis, Chris Fussell, Maggie Holt, and Quinn Wolfe.

Finally, I wish to thank my husband, Curtis (Dick) Smith, whose constant devotion promoted the growth of our marriage even during the most difficult phases of writing this book.

FOREWORD

A dramatic shift in the site of the education of many deaf and hard of hearing children has occured with the advent of PL 94-142 and its accompanying legislation and revisions, interpretations of the meaning of the LRE, mainstreaming, and recently, the inclusionary classroom. These students, once educated in self-contained classes in residential schools or day schools in large public school districts, are now taught in the regular classroom in a neighborhood school.

This shift in site has caused a tremendous change in the traditional role of the teacher of the deaf and hard of hearing from that of a self-contained classroom teacher to that of an itinerant teacher who travels to several schools, and possibly several school districts each day. The competencies required to carry out this new role have also undergone a drastic change. A whole range of new strategies is necessary.

This volume, developed by a practicing itinerant teacher of deaf and hard of hearing students, fills a critical void in the field. It is a source of practical and immediately usable information on the role and responsibilities required of a competent itinerant teacher of the hearing impaired.

Included in the text is information on the duties of an itinerant teacher, the skills and knowledge required, and the organizational skills and some assessment strategies needed. Also contained in this volume is a curriculum designed to prepare a student teacher for the position of an itinerant teacher of the deaf and hard of hearing, including necessary forms and planning documents.

H. William Brelje, Ed. D.
Professor, Coordinator of Special Education: Deaf and Hard of Hearing
Lewis & Clark College, Portland, Oregon

Chapter 1
The Excitement of Itinerant Teaching

One looks back with appreciation to the brilliant teachers, but with gratitude to those who touched our human feelings. The curriculum is so much necessary raw material, but warmth is the vital element for the growing plant and for the soul of the child.

—*Carl Jung*

The Need for Itinerant Teachers

As more and more deaf and hard of hearing students are mainstreamed into the regular classroom, the need grows for specially trained teachers to support these students, their parents, and their regular teachers. Usually there are not enough hearing impaired students in one school to justify a full-time, special teacher on the faculty. Consequently, most special teachers must travel from school to school to serve their mainstreamed students. These teachers are commonly called itinerant teachers of the deaf and hard of hearing. For brevity, this book will often refer to them as "itinerants."

Purposes of this Book

Several kinds of readers may find this book helpful. First, it answers questions of the prospective itinerant teacher of the deaf and hard of hearing. What is it like to do this kind of work? What personal training and characteristics do I need? In addition, experienced itinerants may find some of the instructional tips helpful. Finally, teachers guiding the professional development of itinerant student teachers may find both the first part of the book and the proposed curriculum in Chapter Eight useful as they develop their own local curricula. Whatever your reading purpose, I hope this book leads you toward many exciting experiences with the deaf and hard of hearing.

The Unfolding of Learning

Nothing is more joyful than to witness a child in a moment of discovery. One of those moments came when I put the headphones of an auditory trainer on Willie. His teacher had described his behavior to me, and I suggested that his actions seemed to be that of a deaf child. When he put on the headphones, his eyes lit up and his face took on the most glorious expression I have ever witnessed. Suddenly all our heads with moving lips were making sound! What greater pleasure is there in life than witnessing the moment the world reveals itself in such a new way? It's like that moment in *The Wizard of Oz* when Dorothy opens the door and the world ignites into color.

No Clones in the Classroom!

No two children are alike. Each comes into your life to be respected and nurtured. Most children, if given a proper environment, naturally learn and grow. The teacher aids this process by discovering the strengths and learning style of each child. Our deaf and hard of hearing students are the same as other children, except that they don't hear as well.

One Culture or Two?

The greater a student's hearing loss, the more difficult it will be to learn through hearing, and to communicate by speaking. Yet an appropriate methodology must be discovered to teach him about himself and his world. Sometimes his natural mode of communication will be oral in spite of his disability, sometimes it will be manual (as in American Sign Language), and sometimes a combination of both oral and sign. It can be difficult and time-consuming to discover the most advantageous mode, because each child has a unique history and hearing loss pattern.

Every culture is different. Our children must learn to read and write English because that is our country's language. If the student also learns American Sign Language (ASL), he can become a citizen of two cultures, both the hearing community and the Deaf community which uses ASL.

The Rapture of Discovered Moments

All children are to be honored and nurtured. They are the most important thing! Their growth will come by my being with them daily, tedious as that sometimes is. I teach because I search for the rapture of that single moment when, quite serendipitously, my   student's ignorance unfolds to reveal knowledge. It's the aha! experience. Each time I look into my student's face, he gifts me with something from his soul, either delightful or painful. I am selfish when I consider staying home from work! I would miss those gifts. Without me today, who will create the environment to produce those gifts? As I drive from school to school, I have the luxury of thinking about my students like this.

One Family's Experience

My students' parents also bring me excitement. Although I usually work in a school setting, I collaborate extensively with parents. Knowing the family helps me understand the student better and focus my teaching. Recently I asked several parents to describe their experiences rearing a deaf or hard of hearing child. Suzanne Holt of Portland, Oregon, a parent who is also a speech pathologist, shared the following insights on how an itinerant teacher can help the entire family:

Dear Mary Deane,

Hopefully when a parent is first informed that his/her child is deaf (whether the age of the child be three days, three months, or three years) there should be a support team to work with the family immediately. Having lived in five different states with Maggie, I know firsthand that each state handles the support differently. Ideally a parent-infant trainer is sent to the home and can help the family with their numerous needs. The trainer should understand that the family first must go through a mourning period. The "normal" child they dreamed of has died and the mourning is very real. As with any death, this process cannot be rushed and is very individualized. As soon as the parents are able, the trainer can help process at varying levels. Unfortunately I knew a lot about deafness because of my profession, thus the diagnosis hit me especially hard because I knew how difficult her life would forever be. My husband, on the other hand, thought hearing aids were just like glasses, so it was no big deal. He has since learned gradually of the extreme impact of deafness, and now understands why I was so devastated by the diagnosis.

It is extremely important that the parents become informed! And the itinerant should be that informed person and resource. Help them learn about the hearing aides and what they can and cannot do. But don't stop there. Show them FM units [special assistive learning devices] and the function they have (they don't need to be used in schools only). We bought ours when Maggie was two and I used it when we were inputting language, especially at the zoo, park, etc. Also explain about captioning and all the assistive devices. One reasonably assuring thing for a parent is to be taken on a trip to visit various deaf classrooms. Let the parents see a signing class and an oral class. Find children with a similar loss at various ages and show the parents the progress that is made. In my case the Utah School for the Deaf videotapes all their students yearly, so they could show me various students and how they grew and their speech and language grew with them. And all this in one sitting! We have since videotaped Maggie twice yearly. This helped me to see that indeed she was progressing. Especially in the beginning when progress was agonizingly slow, the videos could demonstrate a change.

The first major decision the parents must make is whether to go with total communication or strictly oral. All itinerants must know that this is the parents' decision, and regardless of their own bias, the parents must choose. The best help the itinerant can be is to inform the parents of the pros and cons of each. Information is what they need! I guess I am saying that the itinerant is not there to just teach the child. The parents are just as important, and need "training" all the way through the years that the child is in training. Informing and motivating the parents as to the needs of the child should actually make the itinerant's job easier, because progress will be a team effort.

An itinerant needs to know that the parents will often be emotional. This isn't just at the beginning, but stays for many years. Often the parents are frustrated and sometimes the itinerants get the brunt of that frustration, even if they are not at all the cause. They are the professionals that the parents are looking to for help and solutions. Try not to take the "outbursts" personally.

The hardest part of having a deaf child is watching the endless struggle to communicate. And because of the lack of communication skills, the endless struggle to try to fit in: to have friends, to understand what is going on, to understand a joke, etc. A deaf child is always left out, maybe not physically, but is left out nonetheless. Never sure of what is happening and why. Never sure of what was just said.

Watching any child grow up and learn all the skills needed for life is a joy, but the joy felt in watching a deaf child is extra sweet. For example, the first time a deaf child places her own order at McDonald's is no ordinary feat, and thus becomes a victory. Selling Girl Scout cookies was no big deal for her sister, but for Maggie, it was also a sweet victory. In other words, each step in progressing toward confidence and independence is looked at with joy and gratitude. Nothing is ordinary.

As hinted above, an itinerant will deal with many emotional issues. So I would recommend at least one class in counseling. How to listen actively and not judgingly. How to give the needed support to the parents and to the child on an emotional level.

Services an itinerant should provide are to inform the parents of resources that might help them as a family (these [resources] need to grow as the child grows); where to get assistive devices; what support groups are in the community; camps that may help; courses that may help (like the support from John Tracy Clinic in Los Angeles); organizations that inform and help (like A. G. Bell Association for the Deaf); and resources the child might enjoy, like computer software that may help teach, HIP magazine for deaf children, etc.

—Suzanne Holt

If you can see yourself helping this parent and teaching her daughter Maggie, read on. The following pages describe the job of itinerant teachers, and what it takes to do it.

Chapter 2

What Itinerant Teachers Do

No other teaching assignment is quite like the job of an itinerant teacher of the deaf and hard of hearing. In the first place, because the itinerant's students occur at a relatively low incidence in the general school population, the teacher must be prepared to work with students in all grades, and in several schools.

The diversity of assignment requires the itinerant to use her car as a traveling office. There is no luxury of classroom storage space, because in most cases we have no single classroom! We take our materials and supplies with us wherever we go. We teach and consult wherever each school's staff can find room for us. Sometimes we get lucky and can work in a real classroom. More often we end up working at a table in the supply room, or just making ourselves and our student comfortable in the hallway. However, an encouraging trend in methodology, known as the inclusion model, is enabling itinerants to spend increasing time in the regular classroom.

In addition to having little control over where she will work, the itinerant some-times has little influence over what will be taught, and when. The curriculum and implementing lesson plans are determined by the school and the regular classroom teacher, whereas the itinerant is only a visiting professional. For this reason it is most helpful for an itinerant to have had previous regular classroom teaching experience.

On the other hand, there are some "perks" for the itinerant as well. Many tradi-tional, time-consuming chores such as recording grades, making out report cards, supervising the lunch room, and changing bulletin boards are refreshingly absent from most itinerants' to-do lists.

Two Kinds of Service

The itinerant provides two major categories of service. All deaf and hard of hearing students receive consultation services, meaning that the teacher provides advice and guidance to school staff and parents, and checks on how students are performing in class, including whether their assistive devices are working appro-priately. A student who is doing well enough in the classroom to need only this first level of observation and consultation service is called a "consult" student.

The second level of service, called "direct serve," includes those students who also need scheduled instruction or tutoring from the itinerant. Direct service implies that the student needs extra support and intervention because of academic, social, or emotional deficits.

Laying the Groundwork

Our service to students always occurs in conjunction with the coordinated efforts of a multidisciplinary team (MDT). Each deaf and hard of hearing student is assigned to an MDT. The MDT is usually composed of one of the student's regular classroom teachers, a speech and language teacher, the itinerant teacher, a school administrator, and a case manager. Membership varies, but the important thing is to gather all the professionals who may be providing the student with service into a single case management group. The team, in cooperation with the student's parents, will develop and review annually an individual education program (IEP) for the student. The IEP prescribes annual academic, social, emotional, and communication objectives that the student should achieve. Levels of professional service to support the student are also prescribed.

Once a deaf or hard of hearing student is assigned to an MDT, the itinerant's work with that student begins. The itinerant often facilitates gathering the information necessary to make the student eligible for service. Here begins the paperwork chase! Needed documents include a hearing evaluation, physician's statement, academic assessment, parental approval, classroom observation, and other documents as the special program and the student's school district require.

After the student has been made eligible for our services, we begin to support the teacher's instruction through various reinforcement strategies. Perhaps we will work in the classroom assisting the teacher, or we will take the student out of the classroom and work with him individually in another space. (Notice I didn't say classroom!) As the itinerant develops a working relationship with the classroom teacher, she will discover ways to be supportive. This can range from providing supplemental materials for a specific topic, to supplying a lesson on hearing loss to the other children, to teaching sign language to all of the students. Each year at least one of my teachers has asked me to teach sign language to her class. We have great fun, all the students develop a greater appreciation of language, and the deaf or hard of hearing student becomes more integrated into the class social structure.

All of the foregoing strategies contribute to positioning the itinerant as a speech and language role model for both the teacher and all her students. In addition, because people fear least that which they know the most about, our students experience less discrimination when a professional in the classroom is able to introduce the facts of hearing impairment.

What It Takes to Be an Itinerant Teacher

1. An Attitude of Flexible Service (How May I Help You?)

Itinerant teachers are above all people of service. Each itinerant teacher brings her own style to this function. But all itinerants look for ways to interact positively and provide services to each of their students, parents, and teachers. For example, while talking with a particular parent, you may need only to serve as a sounding board for all his frustrations, and encourage him to persevere. Or perhaps you notice a student struggling to develop social interaction with his peers; you might offer to work with him by role-playing situations he is likely to encounter. If you approach your job with an attitude of service, you will find a myriad of ways to serve your student, both through direct instruction and by coaching others in your student's life.

At least once every day, and often more frequently, you will need to change something you have planned to accomplish that day. There is no real control over a school's many special events which often conflict with the itinerant's already tight schedule, such as assembly schedules, field trips, and student absences. On a typical day I may be scheduled to provide direct service to only two or three students. That is the day I think I'll have lots of time to catch up on reports, or expedite completion of eligibility documents. But by making one phone call or talking to one parent or staff member, the rest of my day will suddenly be full because I've found some other way to serve my student. Another time I might arrive for my scheduled appointment, only to find my student absent or at an assembly. I have a choice to make. I can react with frustration, or I can choose to stay flexible.

If itinerants remain flexible by continually readjusting schedules and instructional strategies to the needs of classroom teachers and all their students, they can have an impact on deaf and hard of hearing students. The itinerant who is ready to teach any student, anywhere, anytime is one who has the flexibility to impact her students—often in unexpected ways, and at unexpected times. This is part of the excitement of itinerant teaching.

2. Paperwork Organization

Itinerants have a lot of paperwork. Unlike classroom teachers, itinerants need to keep written records of each contact they make with anyone who is involved with a student. So they need to organize carefully, and carry in their car, everything pertaining to each student including the student's IEP, current audiogram, hearing-aid information, classroom teacher's name and phone number, parents' names and phone numbers, and basic office supplies. This will put you in readiness for the unexpected phone call asking about a particular student, such as, "When is Jane's three-year evaluation due date?" If you can answer immediately, you save a trip to the office to look it up in the files, and you also save a return call and possible additional "phone tag." With your records at hand, no matter where you are, you are positioned to simply answer the question and continue on your way.

An extra tip: If you keep a copy of each student's audiogram and vital statistics in your planner, you may not even have to refer to the files in your car. Your planner can also help you keep track of your many commitments and appointments. It's embarrassing to miss a parent or MDT meeting, or to neglect to do something you have agreed to do. In addition, if people perceive you as being disorganized, your credibility and professionalism may be in doubt. On the other hand, if your response time is prompt and you are always on time to meetings, people will be impressed with your caring and your professionalism. Kudos for you!

3. Communication Skills

If you were teaching full-time in a second-grade classroom, your style and vocabulary would remain constant and age-appropriate for second-graders. However, an itinerant teacher is expected to adjust her teaching style and vocabulary with each new student, because she serves kindergarten through community college—sometimes in the same day! Frequently with hard of hearing students, the vocabulary the itinerant or the classroom teacher uses will not be understood. By consistently checking what the student has understood from one's communication, itinerants can adjust their vocabulary and explanations.

Closely related to style and vocabulary level is mode of communication. Some students will be strictly oral, and your modeling of proper speech and syntax will be understood. Other students will be oral but need some ASL signing to clarify what is being said. Still other students will be primarily signers. Sometimes these mainstreamed students will have an interpreter with them during the school day.

Ongoing communication is essential—with the school MDT, the program MDT, your supervisor, school staff (particularly the classroom teacher), the audiologist, and anyone else who interfaces with you regarding a particular student. In addition, never forget to communicate with the parents of your students. Sometimes professionals forget about the needs of the parents. It is they who have the greatest insights into our students. They carry not only the normal burdens of parenting, but also the extra difficulty of rearing a child with a hearing loss. For parents who are actively involved with their child, sometimes the best support an itinerant can give is to let them share their concerns about their child, and to be a liaison between parent and school. Openness and honesty, tempered with caring, will be the best kind of communication.

4. Sensitivity

An itinerant teacher gets many opportunities to be sensitive to others, and without sensitivity she will not be effective in the many roles she plays. Students need to understand that itinerants are aware of their struggles with their hearing loss. Frequently they see itinerants as the only people at school who understand the challenges and difficulties of having a hearing loss.

Itinerants need to be sensitive and supportive of the classroom teacher, too. She has thirty other students and will usually welcome help and support for her children.

Finally, itinerants need to be especially sensitive to the parents. One can only imagine what it is like to be told that your child is deaf. If itinerants are available to the parents and their sensitivity is obvious, parents may become less anxious and more accepting of their child. Their job of making decisions for their child's future will be easier if teachers will listen to them and gently guide them by showing all the options and support available to them.

5. Focus on Student's Need

An itinerant who is not consistently aware of each student's changing needs will not be able to help students cope with the hearing world around them. Oftentimes, hopefully, a student will be able to communicate his changing needs, but sometimes it will be up to the itinerant to notice that something is amiss. In such a case the itinerant will need to either intervene without the student's knowledge, or help the student clarify his need to himself and teach him to advocate for himself.

6. Goals and Objectives

Another skill that itinerants need to develop is the ability to formally and informally assess a student's academic, speech, hearing, and social needs in order to write goals and objectives for the annual IEP and three-year evaluations. These goals and objectives will be the principle guidelines for the coming year. But the real challenge for an itinerant is to go a step further and provide for the other unmeasurable, but equally important, qualities that will help our student grow beyond what is written in the IEP; for example, helping the student learn how to handle troubles at recess or how to take tests. One of the greatest pleasures I have had as an itinerant is when a teacher or parent has shared my delight in an unexpected insight or interaction. Recently I received a message on my voice mail from a speech teacher who exclaimed, "The world has become a wonderful place for Kyle!" Kyle had just been fitted for his first bone-conduction hearing aid, and his speech had become intelligible for the first time. That kind of phone call is a spirit-lifter.

7. Dependability and Credibility

One of the more difficult meetings to arrange is to gather all members of an MDT together, because everyone is operating on a separate schedule and has different deadlines to meet. If you have developed the reputation for doing the research and getting information to people—including the parent—in a timely manner, you will be regarded as a dependable part of the team. However, if you say you will check into a specific concern and fail to fulfill your task, your credibility will suffer, and the reputation of both you and your program will suffer. Service on the MDT requires commitment to your team and consistent follow-though.

8. Training and Experience

Certification requirements for itinerants vary from state to state. Some states do not require the itinerant to have been a regular classroom teacher first. However, I have found that previous regular teaching experience has been immensely helpful to me as an itinerant. I can quickly understand the regular classroom teacher's programs and needs. This helps me integrate service to my special student within the scope of the teacher's total classroom operations.

Another skill area is conversational ability with American Sign Language. How can one possibly meet all the needs of a student who relies on sign, without knowing sign? Yet, amazingly, there are teachers who attempt to enter this work without learning sign. (By the way, you're never too old to learn to sign. I did it at age 50.)

Finally, be sure that your student teaching experience is with a working itinerant teacher. Riding with her from school to school will help you learn the myriad organizational details that are necessary to minimize trivia and maximize your contact with students, teachers, and parents.

Chapter 3
Beginning the School Year

September is an exceptionally busy time. As the school year gets under way, the itinerant teacher renews working relationships with many people. This chapter describes seven key strategies for getting the year off to a fast, productive start.

1. Orient Classroom Teachers Before Students Arrive

The itinerant is well advised to move quickly in the precious few days between the return of teachers and the return of students. While it feels good to return to familiar surroundings and chat casually with colleagues not seen for months, the itinerant must respond to the urgency to orient classroom teachers early. Classroom teachers have only a few days to set up their rooms and get ready for their new students' first day. The itinerant must squeeze into those teachers' busy schedules and brief them on the special students they will have in class. Now is the time for the itinerant to prioritize whom to orient, and to figure out how to do it in a very short time. Here are suggested priorities:

Students Requiring Interpreters The highest priority must be to orient teachers with deaf or hard of hearing students who use interpreters. An interpreter is an expert in American Sign Language hired by the school to translate into sign for the student what the teacher and others are saying in the classroom. The interpreter also speaks in English anything that the student signs. The itinerant must get to these teachers first, to avoid the embarrassment of the interpreter appearing in class the first day of school and the classroom teacher asking, "Who are you?" Orientation, before school begins, is critical for these teachers. The more the teacher understands about deafness and hard of hearing issues, the more comfortable the teacher will be when the interpreter arrives with the deaf or hard of hearing student.

Students Requiring Real Time Captioners Real time captioning is sometimes used for students with severe or profound hearing losses who read well and are less skilled in signing. A relatively new piece of educational technology, the real time caption system is a spin-off from the steno machine long used by court reporters. "Real time captioner" is the job title for a person who operates a real time captioning system. The real time captioner uses machine stenography to input what is being said in the classroom. The output immediately appears in regular English on the student's laptop computer screen. This allows the student to understand what is being said by reading it. In addition, the captioner prepares a printout of the day's transcription and gives it to the student the next day for future reference and study. As with an interpreter, it is essential that the itinerant introduce the captioner to the classroom teacher before the first day of class.

High School Students Because they enroll in several teachers' classrooms, hearing impaired high school students can have numerous accommodation needs, so this group is the itinerant's next priority. A day or two before school begins, the itinerant should hold a group orientation for all of the teachers and staff with whom the student will be interfacing during the year. Practice varies from school to school, but often the student's counselor is willing to call an orientation meeting on behalf of the itinerant. Since counselors usually return to school before the teachers, call your counselors early to request such meetings, perhaps as early as mid-August. If the opportunity for such a meeting is missed, it will be much more difficult to collect teachers and staff together later, and valuable time may have to be spent on individual orientations. The itinerant who has established a rapport with the special education and counseling staff will find it easier to get high school staff together for orientations.

Middle School Students The next priority is orientation of middle school teachers. Again, the itinerant's best bet to facilitate scheduling all of a student's teachers is the counselor, or perhaps someone on the special education staff. While middle school teachers, like high school teachers, are assigned to teach specific subjects, they seem as a group to be more nurturing and willing to attend to the language skill development of a student, regardless of subject taught. Since language is usually the most difficult academic area for deaf and hard of hearing students, the wise itinerant will focus the orientation on language.

Elementary Students Finally, it's important to meet with individual elementary teachers before their students arrive. This is especially true if a student will be using hearing aids, an educational assistant (an aide who does not sign), or an auditory trainer (an FM system requiring the teacher to wear a microphone and transmitter, and the student to wear a receiver and a loop or headphones). The teacher who has not previously worked with deaf or hard of hearing students will feel less anxious when well prepared for the student. Just as important, the teacher is more likely to welcome the itinerant into the classroom if the collegial relationship began before the first day of school.

2. Get Organized the First Week of School

It's a good rule of thumb never to ask to see teachers during the first week of school. They're just too busy. Effective classroom teachers know that the year's classroom behavior and study standards are set in the first few days of school, and they make this their primary focus. So the itinerant wisely uses the first week of school for assembling students' schedules, assessing overall caseload, reviewing student files, and contacting parents. Depending on where the itinerant works, there may also be a student census or a variety of reports that can be either completed at this time, or at least formatted and data collection begun. Like the teachers who are using the first week to set student behavioral routines, the itinerant's use of this week to become highly organized will ensure that the year goes smoothly.

3. Complete Catch-up Orientations

After the first week of school it is appropriate to hold any orientations that couldn't be accomplished before school began. Sometimes, because of the itinerant's large caseload, or because of school schedules, some orientations have to be delayed. When a choice can be made, choose to delay orientations with the teachers of students with mild to moderate hearing losses. Usually, unless a student with a mild to moderate hearing loss wears a hearing aid, the classroom teacher probably hasn't noticed any difference between the regular students and the student with a hearing loss.

4. Perform Student Observations

By the end of the second week of school, the itinerant will have met most of the teachers and school staff, and can begin scheduling student observations. The purpose of observing each student, preferably in a language class, is to watch for teacher, student, and environmental issues. Is the student placed in a suitable environment? Is the teacher using strategies that are adequate for the hard of hearing student to grasp what is being said? Is the environment acoustically adequate for a student using a hearing aid or FM? Is the hard of hearing student using appropriate strategies to gain maximum use of residual hearing and the hearing equipment? The student is appropriately placed when the answer to all these questions is "yes."

If, however, there is concern about any of these issues, now is the time to remedy the situation. For example, the itinerant may need to recommend moving a student to another classroom; or the itinerant might meet with a student's counselor to rearrange the student's whole schedule. If the itinerant is willing to spend time observing and advocating on behalf of the student, the school staff is usually very cooperative. More importantly, a well-placed student is a student ready to learn.

Here's how one student put it:

> I like being in a hearing school because I like to be with kids who can talk because talking is easy for me and I can make more friends. I get to do more active activities and I don't feel like people think I can't do anything. If my deaf friend wanted to be mainstreamed I would say, "It's fun. Don't be shy. Be friendly to others and be active because you won't be pushed around. If you are shy and won't participate with others you'll have a problem."
>
> —Chris Fussell, age 14

5. Review All IEPs and Student Files

Be sure each student has a current individual education plan (IEP) that complies with all laws and regulations. Reading each student's IEP will help the itinerant decide what instruction the direct serve students need. This is the time to schedule direct serve students based on the frequency required by their IEPs, and to put the needs of the consult students on a master to-do list.

There also should be an end-of-the-year form in each student's file from last year, a current audiogram, and other required paperwork. The student file can be used throughout the year to collect student work samples. It's also a good practice to start out the year with a supply of all forms from each school district served. Store in your car two or three copies of each form needed.

6. Begin Direct Service

The time an itinerant teacher spends with direct serve students, one-on-one, in or out of the mainstream classroom, can be the most enjoyable part of the job. The itinerant will normally schedule and begin working with direct serve students by late September. Even when direct service occurs inside the classroom, the itinerant should check with the school secretary to find a place outside the classroom for some one-on-one work. There the itinerant can visually check the direct serve student's hearing aids, as well as check any consult students' aids during unscheduled times at that school.

7. Establish Parent Communication

This is also a good time for the itinerant to contact, by phone or in writing, any parents not spoken with since school started. Give parents your business card, and brief them on the easiest way to reach you. Since most parents of deaf and hard of hearing students do not themselves have hearing losses, voice mail is very popular among parents. Some itinerants also carry pagers. In addition, it's up to each itinerant to decide whether to give parents his or her home phone number. The important point here is that the itinerant needs to establish easy, personal communication early in the year with each parent. If this happens before a problem occurs later in the year, the parent will be more likely to pick up the phone and provide the itinerant with timely information or a timely question. Here's how one parent characterized the communication link:

> The Itinerant Teacher is not the sole source of information for the parents, however, the itinerant teacher must be a source of information. This resource interface role is one of the most important things an itinerant teacher can do. Over time, the itinerant teacher will build a rapport with the parents that is a strong bond of friendship and professional dependency. The itinerant teacher must understand the importance of this role and handle it correctly.
>
> — James Holt

Another parent agreed, adding how the itinerant often develops an intimate relationship with the family:

> The itinerant teacher involved in my son's education was a great asset to our lives from early on. It was really hard at first to decide which educational route to take for my hearing-impaired son. The teacher and programs available helped me to make decisions and feel good about them without guilt. I think the most terrifying obstacle to overcome with a handicapped child is the guilt that maybe you're not doing the "right" thing.
>
> There is no right and wrong, each situation should be handled in an individual manner by the itinerant teacher. A teacher dealing with the child will automatically become a large part of the family. The families will have questions they will be apprehensive about asking, and need to be made to feel

> comfortable to speak to the teacher about anything.
> —Pam Fussell

But not all relationships are guaranteed to be easy and positive. Sometimes the itinerant can do nothing but be a professional listener:

> The itinerant teacher must be a receiver of parental frustrations. There will be many times the parents will unload on the teacher. The parental frustrations may be warranted or not. They may be focused on the itinerant teacher, some other person, or "the system" itself. In any event, the itinerant teacher must put on a "counseling hat" and tough it out. The itinerant teacher must be a solid and professional person who can withstand these (often personal) affronts (at least until the parents are gone and then break into tears). It would be very easy to just say, "I told you so." But the itinerant teacher must remain professional even when the parents become childish. I can remember times when we (as well-educated parents) became childish and let the fur fly. The professional teacher absorbed our frustrations and helped us through it. How do you teach that in school?
> —James Holt

Even just listening sometimes endears the itinerant to a family.

Chapter 4

Orienting Your Teachers

Each September most deaf and hard of hearing students will be assigned to new classroom teachers. Many of these teachers have never taught hearing impaired students and don't understand the implications of even a mild hearing loss. It is the itinerant's responsibility to introduce these teachers to the world of deaf and hard of hearing children. A thoughtful first orientation of the new teacher can be the beginning of a strong collegial relationship and a warm welcome into the classroom. On the other hand, insensitivity to the teacher's time and energy may be viewed as just one more demand upon the already overburdened teacher. What will the itinerant be able to do for the student without a welcome into the classroom? The tenor of the student's whole year is set by the itinerant's early interaction with the classroom teacher.

First Contacts

The itinerant usually starts meeting new staff and teachers before school actually begins. If a student is deaf, uses an FM, has more than one teacher, or is in middle or high school, try to have a brief meeting with the teacher to introduce yourself and set an orientation time—always at the teacher's convenience—when you can get together and review the student's audiogram and special needs. Sometimes the teacher has time at that moment, and the brief contact expands into the actual orientation. If not, make a return appointment, preferably before school begins. During this brief meeting also ask the teacher how you may be of help in making the adjustment to instructing a deaf or hard of hearing student. The teacher needs to learn that you are there to help, not to dump more work on her.

If the teacher seems relaxed and willing to spend more time learning about hearing losses in your first brief meeting, give her some useful handouts, such as a list of teaching strategies. If the teacher seems very busy or under stress, acknowledge that and tell her you will leave some papers in her mailbox to read when she has some quiet time. This last strategy is the least desirable, but, particularly if you can't orient the teacher before the student begins class, you at least want her to have some information readily available. It would be unfair to have a student with a hearing loss show up the first day of school with the teacher wondering what to do with this "deaf kid."

Planning the Orientation

Each orientation must adjust to the particular needs of the individual teacher. For example, a teacher inexperienced with the deaf and hard of hearing may need a very comprehensive orientation, while the experienced teacher may need only a briefing on the specific needs of a student new to her classroom. Here are the major topics to cover in a comprehensive orientation:

- Getting to Know the Classroom Teacher
- Explaining the Student's Audiogram
- Reviewing the Language/Learning Connection
- Explaining Swiss Cheese Learning
- Sharing Instructional Strategies
- Facilitating Test Taking
- Explaining Services the Itinerant Can Provide
- Offering to Provide a Classroom Presentation

Presenting the Orientation

Getting to Know the Classroom Teacher

The first person to orient is yourself. You can quickly and unintentionally become an intruder in the classroom if you don't understand the teacher. Take time to get acquainted. Each teacher you serve is naturally possessive of her students and her classroom. Therefore, approach your relationship as if you were a guest in her home. Familiarize yourself with her teaching philosophy and classroom strategies. It is your responsibility to make a good first impression. Both in the orientation and later when you enter her classroom, be sure that the teacher perceives you as a professional in dress and manners, and as a person who is here only to help her— not to tell her how to teach or manage her classroom. Cooperation is the key to your student getting the necessary services. Establish a good relationship with your teacher, and you will always have access to your student!

Explaining the Student's Audiogram

A teacher who encounters an audiogram for the first time may be overwhelmed by the amount of information displayed. So after showing what the student's completed audiogram looks like (see Figure 4.1), do the remainder of the orientation from a graphic audiogram informally called a "speech banana" (see Figure 4.2). The speech banana shows what everyday sounds, including speech sounds, occur at various loudness and frequency levels. Point out to the teacher that speech sounds are the softer sounds in the 20 to 60 decibel range, and occur in a roughly banana-shaped area in the top half of the graphic audiogram.

The pictorial layout of the speech banana helps focus the teacher's attention quickly on the kinds of sounds the student will not be able to hear. The student's hearing loss is normally plotted on the graphic audiogram in two colors, red for the right ear and blue for the left ear. In Figure 4.2, however, "0" is used for the right ear and "X" is used for the left ear. The student can hear only sounds below the plotted line for each ear. Wherever the line falls below a spoken sound in the speech banana, the student has a hearing impairment that may have instructional implications.

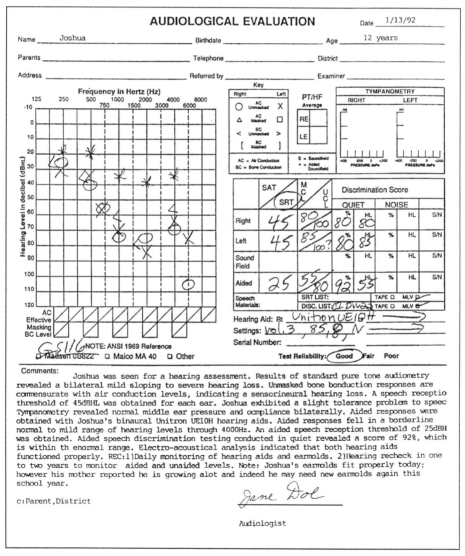

Figure 4.1

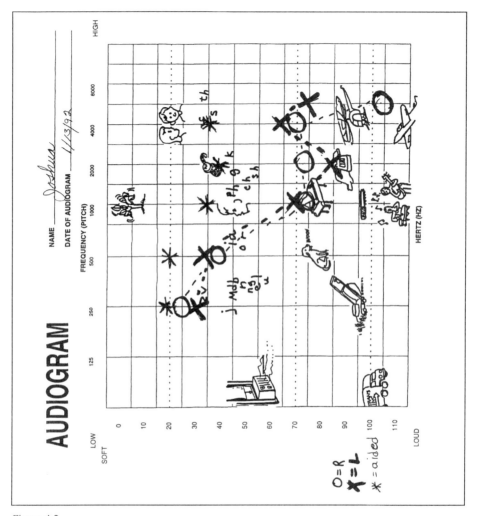

Figure 4.2

Reviewing the Language/Learning Connection

Regular classroom teachers already know that we learn through language. However, they sometimes need to be reminded of this language/learning relationship, and have it pointed out to them that signing and speechreading are just two alternative modes of language that can be used for learning. A great variety of alternative language/learning modes exists, as the National Council of Teachers of English Commission on Composition pointed out in 1986:

When people articulate connections between new information and what they already know, they learn and understand that new information better. When people think and figure things out, they do so in symbol systems commonly called languages, most often verbal, but also mathematical, musical, visual, and so on. When people learn things, they use all of the language modes to do so . . . reading, writing, speaking (signing) and listening (seeing); each mode helps people learn in an unique way. When people write about new information and ideas, they learn and understand them better. When people care about what they write and see and are able to make connections to their own lives, they both learn and write better.

Since deaf and hard of hearing students are the equals of hearing students in all other respects, the itinerant will be responsible for showing the classroom teacher ways to help the student acquire language and learning.

Explaining Swiss Cheese Learning

The next stage in orienting the teacher is to explain "Swiss cheese learning." Ideally, through the use of both speechreading and assistive hearing devices, the student with a hearing loss would be able to receive all the spoken language that a person with regular hearing receives. Unfortunately, the hearing process doesn't work that neatly. A student with good speechreading skills and a well-fitted hearing device will typically still miss some sounds. Here's how a spoken sentence might be received by a student with a moderate to severe hearing loss, aided with a hearing aid to 35db:

How a Sentence Is "Heard" by a Student with a Hearing Loss
(Simplified Illustration)

A. Spoken Sentence by Teacher: "Find the sentence that shows how Carla felt."

B. Sounds Heard by Student: " ind e en en   a show how arla el ."

C. Sounds Speechread by Student: "F   th s   th show how arl f   ."

The person with regular hearing hears the full sentence (line A). But the student with the hearing loss has to combine both the sounds heard through the hearing aid (line B) and the sounds that are speechread (line C). Even then the student does not receive all the spoken sounds, yet some teachers assume that hearing aids combined with speechreading enable a student to hear all sounds. (After all, don't eyeglasses pick up all the light?) Furthermore, speechreading may not be even as efficient as line C would make it appear; in reality, a good speechreader may have only partial success at picking up the first "s" sound and the "h" sound in "how." The student attempts to make sense of what is said by piecing together perceived bits and parts of speech, supplemented by whatever can be surmised from the speaker's physical appearance and the situational context.

What happens with most students is that the hearing aid is only partially effective, and speechreading, while helpful, doesn't catch everything being lost by the aid. Thus B + C still comes up short of equaling A. The student "hears" a communication, but it has gaps and holes in it, like Swiss cheese. In turn, the language/learning connection is impacted, so most students with hearing losses wind up with Swiss cheese learning. How large the gaps in learning are is determined by how much the hearing aid doesn't receive, and how much of that loss isn't picked up in speechreading.

But it gets even more complicated. Swiss cheese learning seems to consume even more time than regular learning. Not only does the student have to match words against information already in the memory, but gaps in this information must also be compared against previously stored gaps. (This is why rapid oral instruction by the teacher should be avoided; give the student time to process.) Sometimes a mistake is made in the processing, and the brain stores the right information in the wrong place, which is why it is common for students with hearing losses to make a comment that is completely unrelated to the topic. That's a Swiss cheese response; the student is retrieving a misfiled learning.

Other critical causes of gaps in learning are distractions and fatigue. If the student looks away for a moment, he misses the input available from speechreading (remember line B above?). If he becomes fatigued, he will begin to miss vital contextual clues. And when he gives up listening to follow-up discussion by the students, he misses reinforcement of the knowledge. More gaps. More Swiss cheese.

Sharing Instructional Strategies

The first barrier to the regular classroom teacher's effective instruction is the illusion that the student appears "to hear." In fact, the student can probably "hear" something, but the sounds may not be identical to what most persons with regular hearing hear. If you have a tape or film that portrays the experience of hearing at various levels of hearing loss, this is an effective place to share it.

Once the teacher believes that the student has difficulty hearing, she must be helped to understand that all instruction must capitalize on what aided hearing the student does have, plus his current skill in speechreading. The following are some suggested instructional strategies for the classroom teacher.

Where You Stand

The student needs to see your face for speechreading.

Face the class when you talk, not the board. Keep the light in your face, not in the student's eyes.

Be careful not to stand in front of the windows.

Avoid moving around excessively; the student may have difficulty seeing your face.

How You Speak

Talk naturally, at a slightly slower pace than usual.

Avoid unnatural lip movement.

Always speak with your mouth uncovered.

Use whole sentences to give contextual clues, and to provide a language model.

How You Teach

Prepare your student before class by briefly discussing the lesson.

Set high but realistic expectations.

Provide a notetaker for the student, if needed.

Be sure your student is watching before you speak or give assignments.

Ask open-ended comprehension questions, so the student can't respond with a yes or no.

Encourage the student to answer in full sentences; this helps you check comprehension.

Encourage the student to ask for repetition or rephrasing when he needs it.

Rephrase misunderstood statements; you may have said words he can't speechread.

Name each speaker, so the student knows who is talking.

Cue your student to page numbers in the textbook.

Do not confuse attempts at manipulation with naiveté and poor social skills.

Review the student's progress frequently.

Accommodating Your Student's Physical Needs

Realize the student can't understand everything from speechreading.

Recognize that speechreading is tiring; provide opportunities for breaks.

Allow the student to move so that he can speechread the speaker.

Using Media

Write new and unusual words on the board.

Write homework assignments on the board.

Use the board or an overhead to draw attention to key points.

Use an overhead outline or printed handout to assist students in following presentations.

Keep the room light enough for speechreading, if needed.

Avoid talking while using media with sound.

Provide the student with a script or written summary of filmed material.

Share your own notes with the student.

Use hands-on experiential activities frequently.

Facilitating Test Taking

It is common to hear from teachers that a student with a hearing loss has difficulty scoring well on tests. The student seems to know the information, does well with homework assignments, and answers questions correctly in class, but the written test scores are lower than expected. There are four typical reasons for this phenomenon:

What Test? The student might not have "heard" there was going to be a test and therefore didn't study for it. If this happens the student and teacher should work out a daily system for getting assignments.

Wrong Information The student knew about the test, studied hard, but studied the wrong information. If no written outline was presented in class on what the test would cover, or if the areas that the students should have studied were not stressed in class, the student may not have known how or what to study and therefore concentrated on unimportant information. If this happens the teacher should talk to the student about how he prepared for the test. If his preparation was misguided, plan some sort of review system with him prior to future tests, and stress the areas of study upon which the student needs to concentrate.

Vocabulary Deficit Unfamiliar vocabulary in a test question may cause the student to answer incorrectly. Be sure to use words in the test which have previously been introduced to the student.

Lack of Effort Finally, the student knew about the test but didn't study enough. This can happen to any student, hearing or deaf. If this is the case the student should be treated as you would treat any of your other students.

Getting the Information to the Students A student with a hearing loss needs to learn to answer regular test questions the same as anyone else. But the student may need help in understanding what information the test questions are asking. There are several ways to provide this help without disrupting the testing procedure during class:

- The teacher can write the test questions in the usual way. When she passes out the test she can go over the ones that might be confusing to the student with the hearing loss. Students can be called on to explain what the question is asking. This brief discussion and simplification might help all the students without singling out the student with the hearing loss.

- The teacher can pass out the test and tell the class to begin, then go to the hard of hearing student and ask him to explain in his own words what each of the more difficult questions means. If he can explain the question satisfactorily, he can proceed. If he is confused, the teacher will need to rephrase or simplify the question.

- If the classroom situation doesn't allow enough time to do either of the above, the teacher can do one of the following: 1) The student can take the test after school with the teacher, when he can ask for clarification as needed. 2) The teacher can send a copy of the test to the resource room for another person to administer. 3) The teacher can write a simplified version of the more difficult words and phrases right on the student's copy of the test, and allow him to take the test with the other students.

Explaining Services the Itinerant Can Provide

Toward the end of your orientation, be sure to describe the many services which you can either provide personally or obtain through referral. The inexperienced teacher may be unaware of everything you are capable of doing to support the student. Services to mention at this point include:

- Teaching small groups in the classroom
- Individual and group instruction in sign language
- Hearing tests
- Hearing-aid evaluations
- Hearing-aid maintenance, checkup, and repairs
- Trial use of assistive aids, such as FM and real time captioning
- Consultation with professional staff
- Consultation with parents
- Coordination of community resources

Taken together, these services can be combined effectively to help the student succeed in the classroom. Here's how one student put it:

> What I like about being in a hearing school is having lots of friends and the short bus ride. What I don't like about the hearing school is not knowing any of the songs in the music class and I need to learn them. It has lots of hard work and sometimes it's too hard having hearing friends. Sometimes in class I can't see who is talking so I can't follow the discussion.
>
> My itinerant teacher helped me with some vocabulary words and helped me to talk about some problems that I have. My itinerant was my friend. The itinerant can also help explain things that are going on in the classroom or school.
>
> If my deaf or hard of hearing friends wanted to go to my school I would tell them about my school. Also that they need to work hard and not give up. They'll probably enjoy it. If some kids tease them, they need to ignore it.
>
> The itinerant can help tell the classroom teacher what the deaf child needs. Like don't talk too fast. Don't use too many hard words. Answer lots of questions, like what that word means. Help the deaf child enjoy school and be happy. The deaf child will need lots of things explained.
>
> One day I missed the bus. I went to the office and told the lady. She said to just call home. I told her I couldn't call. She said have a friend show you how. I had to say, "No, I can't call because I am deaf!"
>
> —Maggie Holt, age 12

Offering to Provide a Classroom Presentation

Finally, some itinerants offer to do a follow-up "dog and pony show" with all the teacher's students. Geared to the group's age level, the purpose of the student orientation is to acquaint hearing students with the nature of hearing losses. The orientation should include a description of how we hear, how hearing can be damaged, what it's like to have a hearing loss, and some of the typical behaviors of persons with hearing loss. The itinerant can use lots of hands-on experiences. The students can handle hearing aids, ear molds, and an FM. The itinerant can show them a large ear model or picture of the parts of the ear. An audiotape that allows students to experience various levels of hearing loss can be played.

A thorough orientation is time well spent. When it becomes OK to talk about hearing losses in class—perhaps even with participation by the student who has a loss—the students feel less awkward about having someone in class who seems different. Most important, the hearing students are more likely to befriend than tease. Teasing is a common problem experienced by hearing impaired students, even by this high school senior who is the best javelin athlete in Oregon:

> In my regular high school I have done well, both in sports and school. Being in a 4A level in sports has made me the best-in-state javelin. A regular school offers more varieties of everything. But . . . when I misunderstand something, mispronounce something, or I do something stupid some of the kids tease me because I'm deaf. But, only because I'm deaf they don't understand me.
>
> —Kevin Davis, age 17

People tend to fear what they don't understand. The itinerant's orientation of a class can promote understanding and thereby reduce the amount of teasing experienced by these students.

Orientation's Payoff: A Motivated Classroom Teacher

A well-oriented teacher saves the itinerant many needless, time-consuming crises later in the school year. Most teachers enjoy having a student with a hearing loss in class, once they understand the disability, how to work with it, and how to recognize the small steps of progress the student will make. Sometimes the teacher becomes extraordinarily absorbed in the learning adventures of the student with a hearing loss. Here is a letter from a classroom teacher who had such an experience:

> I hope I've been able to teach Quinn as much as he's taught me. Of the two of us, I've probably had more fun. We've both

worked very hard, and we've shared frustration that bloomed into discovery and lots of laughter along the way.

Quinn has a wonderful sense of humor and is very bright, particularly if you define intelligence as problem solving. His problem is that he hates using his FM. The school has taken the position that it is imperative that he use the device, on the odd chance that he might hear something. Quinn feels that hearing is substantially overrated, since the odd squawks and funny buzzing sounds that the device brought to him were not useful sounds. He still could not hear anything of value to him unless you count the day that a front-end loader dropped its load outside our classroom window, causing the earth to shake and making a very low frequency, very loud sound. Quinn jumped and yelled, "What tha . . . .?"

For instructional use, however, the FM did indeed seem to be of little value and a source of irritation to Quinn. So, he "forgot" it daily and had to go get the spare one in another classroom. This errand could be stretched to ten minutes, and since he is quite social, it generally was ten minutes. Then he "forgot" to turn it on, though he would tell me it was on, that it was working, when in fact he very often didn't have the cords connected. When caught in these minor indiscretions, he would smile or laugh and shrug his shoulders. You'd think he was a kid.

Early this school year, I passed out a health questionnaire to all of my classes, the goal being to discover individual needs early and meet them more effectively. There were questions such as "Do you often get headaches?" and "Can you see the chalkboard clearly from your seat?" When Quinn came to "Do you have trouble hearing?" he marked "No." I laughed as I realized he is right. He has no trouble hearing. He has trouble with people who expect him to hear!

—Marilyn Pardes

Chapter 5

Meeting Your Students' Hearing Needs

Hearing support is a large part of what we do for our parents and students. Our mainstreamed students frequently are the only deaf or hard of hearing students in their schools. Consequently, there is often no on-site specialized support, and the itinerant becomes the student's liaison for services related to hearing loss.

Documentation Needed for Service

Typically, the child with a hearing loss comes to the itinerant teacher with a file of paperwork. Documentation may include:

- Parent permission to evaluate student
- Request for program services (sometimes called a "referral")
- Audiogram from a certified audiologist
- Physician's statement
- Statement of eligibility for program services
- Current individual education plan (IEP) for grades K-12
- An individual family plan (IFP) from the preschool years
- Parent consent for initial placement in special education

Preschool Services

Sometimes the student's needs have been well met before kindergarten. In many areas funded services now exist for very young children with hearing losses. If the student is lucky, someone will have noticed the child's hearing loss and requested an evaluation as early as age two. While the details are outside the scope of this book, many such programs employ preschool itinerant teachers who deliver services to deaf and hard of hearing preschoolers in their homes. The earlier the child is fitted with hearing aids and begins to receive service, the easier it will be to absorb language and maximize readiness for entry into elementary school.

K-14 Services

In many school districts, if the student enters a school with all the paperwork in place, the admitting secretary will usually notify the itinerant of the student's enrollment. If the student has not been served previously by a hearing specialist, the notification may come from a speech and language pathologist who has been working with the student on referral from the classroom teacher. The itinerant's first step is to perform a structured observation of the student in the classroom to observe behavior, listen to the student's speech, and make a preliminary estimate of appropriateness of placement. Next, the itinerant interviews the pathologist, parents, and teacher to collect more information about how the student is functioning. Finally, if it appears the student needs service, the itinerant begins the process of enrolling the student into the deaf and hard of hearing program by assembling a file of information similar to the list above. This means the itinerant also recommends and sometimes coordinates the needed professional examinations, or encourages others to do so.

Creating the IEP

After an audiologist has evaluated the student, a copy of the audiogram with a recommendation for appropriate amplification systems is sent to the parents, the case manager, and the itinerant. Then, in consultation with the parents, the school multidisciplinary team (MDT) creates an IEP for the student, or amends the existing IEP. Special circumstances may also require ratification of the IEP changes by the district or regional MDT. Finally, direct service or consultation service by the itinerant will commence.

Getting Amplification for the Student

Although most students with hearing losses will benefit from amplification, this is not always the case. Whether or not the audiologist has determined that the student will benefit from amplification, the itinerant serves as a consultant to the parents, teacher, and school staff. Usually a "consult" student has a mild or unilateral (one ear only) hearing loss which does not interfere with academic, social, or emotional growth. Some of these children automatically adjust their learning styles to meet their needs, but others need to be taught about their hearing loss, and how to maximize their residual hearing.

If the audiologist recommends hearing aids or an auditory trainer (FM system), the itinerant will work with the student on a number of hearing technology issues. For example, the itinerant may:

- Request an annual hearing evaluation by a certified audiologist
- Check the hearing aid and its mold, both visually and by listening to it
- Check the hearing aid electroacoustically with a hearing-aid analyzer
- Make minor repairs to the aid, or send it to the audiologist for more difficult repairs

Delivering Itinerant Services

For each student identified as having academic, social, or emotional needs related to a hearing loss, the itinerant teacher provides either consultation or instruction to help the student make progress. Services are in accordance with the student's IEP. Instruction is usually three times or less per week in a mainstreamed classroom. (Where three times is not enough, the student may need to be placed in a self-contained classroom for students with hearing losses.) The itinerant's range of services for each student may include one or more of the following:

Consultation Services

- Participate in IEP and MDT meetings
- Write reports for the MDT, other staff, and parents
- Request an annual hearing evaluation by a certified audiologist
- Check the hearing aid and its mold, both visually and by listening to it
- Check the hearing aid electroacoustically with a hearing-aid analyzer
- Make minor repairs to the aid, or send it to the audiologist for more difficult repairs
- Orientation, advice, and coaching to the student's parents
- Orientation, advice, and coaching to the student's classroom teacher
- Orientation, advice, and coaching to other professional staff
- Advocate the student's needs to other agencies and potential employers

Direct Instructional Services

- Coaching in the use of hearing aids and FM systems
- Individual instruction outside the classroom
- Individual instruction in the regular classroom
- Group instruction in the regular classroom, including the student with a hearing loss
- Field trips into the community, and to employer sites
- Language development
- Auditory training

Follow-Up Services

The itinerant also provides an orientation to the students' teachers and support staff regarding hearing loss and the amplification systems that the student uses. Included in these orientations may be recommendations for classroom modifications, curriculum or instructional modifications, and communication or language modifications. Sometimes the itinerant will provide written resource or curriculum materials. The itinerant is also available for classroom presentations upon request by the teacher and with the approval of the student and parents.

Whether the itinerant provides consultation or direct instructional services, all assigned students' hearing aids must be checked as needed and, three times a year, each aid's functioning should be measured with a hearing-aid analyzer.

When done well, the delivery of these services gets results. In the following letter, the parent of a middle school student described her son's successful adaptation to the classroom:

> Then he got the match made in heaven. It was not only the services he received directly from his new teacher, it was how the itinerant mobilized the faculty at the middle school. He was one of the first deaf students at the middle school and nobody felt competent to work with the hearing-impaired. The staff felt that was the work of the itinerant but the new teacher reassured all my son's teachers that all of the staff could help him in some way. In a few months, my son went from the class clown, often cruelly mimicking students with more severe handicaps, to actually being a student assistant in a computer

class. On the last day of school the special education teacher was wishing my son and another girl good luck in high school. My son chimed in, "Yeah, more people will like you [the student] if you are nice." I thought, how introspective. He went from Mr. Know-It-All to accepting advice and realizing the importance of socialization.

—Marie Wolfe

Chapter 6

Organizing Your Office on Wheels

The Right Car

A reliable car is absolutely essential for the itinerant teacher. Not only does the car get the itinerant from school to school quickly throughout the day, but it also doubles as a storeroom for records and teaching materials. Almost any car can be made to work as an itinerant's office, but many teachers prefer a four-door sedan with front bucket seats separated by a console. This configuration enables easy access to materials on the back seat, either by reaching over the console, or through a rear door. For inclement days, the ability to reach conveniently over the console can be a definite advantage.

Transportation Expenses

Use of a car on the job means you will be incurring out-of-pocket expenses. Most employers will reimburse you for the mileage you drive on the job. When you consult your tax advisor on this matter, you will probably find that your reimbursement checks are not reportable as state or federal income. This is because most employers reimburse at or below the maximum rate permitted by the Internal Revenue Service. The maximum rate presumably covers your cost of gasoline, insurance, repairs, and even capital depreciation.

Nevertheless, you may be facing an insurance premium hike because your car is used on the job. First, calculate how many miles you think you will be driving on the job in a 12-month period (don't count mileage at the beginning and end of each day between home and work). Then check with your insurance agent. Some insurers will not charge an additional premium if the annual mileage is less than an amount established by that company. If your insurer does want to charge an additional premium, it may be to your advantage to shop around before purchasing on-the-job coverage.

Next, let's consider what to keep inside your car. Don't underestimate the crucial role your car will play in your work! You'll save yourself mountains of frustration by having the materials described below on board when you leave your garage each morning.

The Box System

How conveniently and quickly materials can be retrieved and assembled in the car can greatly influence how well the teaching day goes. Use large plastic file boxes with handles, hinged lids, and rounded edges to store all materials. These boxes are now readily available in the plastic storage goods sections of large markets and home stores. Choose the kind that is about 12 inches on each side. Select colors that complement your upholstery—you'll be seeing a lot of them! Position two boxes in the rear seat so that the lids open toward the front seat.

Student File Box

The first box should contain a working file for each student, including the current IEP, a sample of the student's work, an audiogram, and the audiogram transposed onto a speech banana so it will be easier for the hearing staff to visualize what the student can and cannot hear. With these files always at hand, the itinerant is always ready to discuss a student in depth, as well as plan instruction.

Forms and Information Box

In the second box keep blank copies of any other forms and information sheets that might be needed. These come from your program office and the districts in which you work, and are used for requesting various services, informing teachers, and counseling parents. This can turn out to be a surprisingly large number of materials! Typical forms and information sheets that the itinerant needs to retrieve quickly include:

Forms
- Audiograms
- Eligibility for Service
- FM Evaluation
- FM Request
- IEP Forms, by District
- Mileage Reimbursement Form
- Observation of Student
- Request for Services
- Request for FM System
- Speech Bananas
- Teacher Evaluation of Child with Identified Hearing Loss
- Transition Planning
- Triennial Reevaluation

Information Sheets
- Community Resources
- Consult and Direct Services
- Effects of Hearing Loss
- Hearing Aid Maintenance
- Real Time Captioning Information
- Sign Language
- Speech: What Is It?
- Warm Fuzzies for Myself/Inspiration
- Working with Interpreters

Place several copies of each item in its own file folder. Keep these folders arranged alphabetically, or in some other order that facilitates quick retrieval.

The Daily Box

Place a third box in the front passenger seat, positioned so it opens toward the driver. This is your "Daily Box," where today's paperwork is staged, so you can review the materials before entering a particular school. Items may include today's daily work for each individual student; a kit with hearing aid tools and supplies; and anything else that may be needed, including a plastic bag filled with pencils, colored felt pens (crayons melt too easily), tape, glue, erasers, small stapler, paper clips, scissors, a small ruler, and anything else you might use while working with a student.

Finally, itinerant work generates excess paper! If you don't like a messy car, keep a little plastic recycle bin on the floor behind the passenger seat. You will probably need one that's long and narrow. Measure the available floor area, and shop for a size that's slightly smaller and is compatible in color with your boxes. You'll be surprised at how much trash will accumulate, particularly if you eat lunch in your car. At the end of each day, just empty the trash into your home recycling bin.

It's crucial to keep the paperwork and trash organized, or you'll lose time with the kids!

Music

Visualize yourself rushing to your next student—hurriedly parking your car—rushing into the school—signing in at the office—having a wonderful lesson planned—and the secretary saying, "I'm sorry, your student is absent today!"

Time to regroup. What better way than to retreat to your car, turn on your favorite music, and spend a quiet hour doing paperwork while you fill your soul with music?

Food

Your glove compartment can be a pantry. Keep a supply of snack foods in there, such as individually wrapped, fat-free granola bars or raisins. Experienced itinerants eat something before late afternoon meetings to prevent that sluggish, tired feeling. In addition, your car is sometimes a lunchroom. While it helps to use lunchtime in the faculty dining room to develop your relationships with a school's staff, sometimes that isn't convenient. Alternatively, you may want to write during that quiet time when you are sitting in your car and eating lunch. On the days when that quiet time gets gobbled up by a meeting or student, you can at least grab something from your "pantry" to keep you going until you can get a meal. And consider scheduling a monthly lunch at a restaurant with other itinerants, just to stay in touch.

Dress and Grooming

Itinerant teachers interface with many people each day, so it's important to be well groomed. You may need to dress a little more formally than most classroom teachers, for in addition to your teaching role at each school, you have a consulting role. Experienced consultants know that professional dress makes a professional impression and maintains credibility of the program they represent. Your box in the passenger seat is a good place to keep grooming materials, so you can freshen up before entering each school.

Personal Planner

The control center for your activities should reside in your personal planner. Many successful itinerants, realizing their activities are similar to those of business people on the move, have adopted such business-oriented planners as the Franklin Day Planner, Day Timer, or Day Runner. If you don't already own one of these, inspect them at a nearby stationery or specialty store and consider adopting one. Not only will you be able to track your variable instructional schedule and meetings, but you will also have a convenient place to keep basic information on all your students.

In addition, when you get paged, you will often be able to save yourself a trip to your car. Does your program secretary want to know the date of Jane's next IEP? Just open your planner to your student data section. You've avoided dashing out through the rain to the parking lot to pull the full file on that student.

The following is a sample of a student information sheet. It can be formatted to 5 1/4″ x 8 1/2″, to fit in a standard personal planner.

STUDENT INFORMATION SHEET

IEP REVIEW DATE ____/____/____

3-YEAR EVALUATION ____/____/____

NAME _____

BIRTHDATE _____ ID# _____

CASE MGR _____

PHONE _____

TEACHER/COUNSELOR _____

PHONE _____

SCHOOL _____GRADE _____

DISTRICT_____

LAST AUDIOLOGY EXAM ____/____/____

HEARING LOSS _____

AIDED: YES NO // OWN LOAN // LOAN# _____

RT EAR MODEL _____ # _____

LT EAR MODEL _____ # _____

PARENT _____

ADDRESS _____ APT _____

_____ ZIP _____

PHONE   DAYTIME _____

NIGHT _____

In addition to the student information sheet, I include the following handy items in my planner:

- Personalized stationary, 5 1/4" x 8 1/2"
- Business cards
- Pens and pencils
- Post-It notes
- Paper clips
- Rubber bands
- Band-aids
- A nice supply of stickers—even high schoolers and teachers enjoy receiving them!
- A record of each contact I make with a student, teacher, other staff, or parent (use your planner's "customer contact" form—it's designed for salespersons, but works equally well for itinerant work)

Chapter 7

....

Ending The School Year

Like late spring mountain runoffs, the last six weeks of school are highly fluid. Students go on field trips with their classes, participate in spring program rehearsals, and the like. Most of the IEPs, triennial evaluations, and transition meetings have been completed, and the itinerant, having survived the whitewaters of meeting mania, can flow quietly through the instructional schedule. The school year is almost finished, but a few items of business must still be accomplished.

Follow Through to the Last Day

The highest priority is to continue serving students, teachers, and parents until the last day of the term. Avoid the temptation to use the many spring activities as excuses to ease off; maintain your flow of regular service until the last day. When students are not available for your scheduled direct service, use these precious chunks of time to write the year-end reports on a laptop computer. Be sure to deliver a year-end report to each student's file, so that next year's classroom teacher can review the student's learning status in August or early September. Such a report may seem needless, if one assumes that the same itinerant will be serving the student again next year. However, the student may enroll in a new school, another itinerant may take on that student, or the next classroom teacher may want to review the status of incoming students before meeting with the itinerant in September.

On the following page is a handy format for a year-end report, which an itinerant could place on computer and individualize for each student. The format is an adaptation of one currently in use by the Columbia Regional Program for the Deaf and hard of hearing, administered by the Portland Public Schools on behalf of school districts in northwest Oregon.

[Name of School District, or Special Hearing Program]
[Address and Phone Number Where Itinerant Teacher Can Be Reached]

1996-97 YEAR-END STUDENT REPORT

Student Name: Jane B. Doe   **Report Date:** June 4, 1997

Student Number: 422 534 906   **District:** John Muir Unified
Date of Birth: 1/26/84   **School:** Lincoln
Grade: 6

Level of Service: Direct   **Itinerant Teacher:** Mary Deane
Smith
Intervention Units Provided: 47   **Case Manager:** Indira Ngwama
IEP Due Date: 5/26/98   **Triennial Evaluation Date:** 5/26/99

Date of Last Hearing Test: 1/13/97
Right Hearing Aid: Unitron UE10H   **Left Hearing Aid:** Unitron UE10H
Use of Other Amplification: FM

Other Special Education Services Provided:
     Speech/Language Yes: No: X   **Provider's Name:**
     Academic   Yes: X   No: **Provider's Name:** Resource Room

Orientations of School Staff: An orientation was done and copies of teaching strategies were left with her teacher on 9/8/96.

Additional Information/Classroom Observations: Jane became direct serve, two times per week, in January, 1996.

Plans to be Implemented, Fall 1997: Jane will be entering Madison Middle School in September. A staff orientation needs to be done before school starts in September. Jane will need considerable academic support.

Stanford Achievement Test, Hearing Impaired Edition:

Subject	Date Administered	Grade Level Equivalent	Percentile Rank Hearing Impaired
Reading	March 1997	4.7	72
Language	March 1997	3.0	53
Vocabulary	March 1997	3.0	Not normed for HI
Math	March 1997	4.5	37

Wrap Up Your Personal Contacts

Maintain good interpersonal relations by meeting one last time in June with everyone:

- Say good-bye to each student.
- Thank every classroom teacher for a year of professional cooperation.
- Thank each support staff person in each school, such as principals and secretaries.
- Thank program administrators and colleagues, such as the audiologist.
- Give each parent equipment repair phone numbers for the summer.

It's OK to spend time visiting with all these people! Building effective relationships with everyone is important because, in the long run, it makes service easier. When an itinerant encounters a particularly difficult situation, having everyone's understanding and support already in place can ensure a speedy and effective solution for the student.

We do not celebrate our successes enough. End-of-year is a good time to look back and assess how far you've come with your students. Get your colleagues and parents to spend a little time doing this, too. It's a great re-enforcer. Here's what one parent wrote in reviewing her son's progress:

> The successes [for my son] have been many. From ... when he ordered his first ice cream cone by himself in the ice cream store, to going off to school for the first time. I'm happy that he has "broken the mold" for hearing-impaired kids. Even though he went to school twelve miles away, he played sports in his neighborhood, and made friends in his neighborhood as well as at school. He has done very well academically, consistently making the honor roll. He has been to three schools before entering the high school he is now attending. In each school he made friends, did well in class, and showed kids what a hearing-impaired kid could do. That he was just like them in most ways, and special in others. He has worked twice as hard as his other friends and classmates to attain equal or better results. We have been very happy when he has been recognized for his efforts in sports, where he could excel

on an individual and team level. He has had many opportunities to speak before other students and some adult groups. When he finishes his speech I feel especially proud of him.

—Elaine Davis

An Afterthought About What Really Happens During Summer Vacation

I always have intentions of neatly filing all my personal paperwork into appropriate files before I leave for summer, but I have never yet accomplished this. By the last day of work all I can think about is freedom and beginning summer. So I throw everything into my boxes, stash them in a dark closet, and don't think about them until the final week of vacation. When I am feeling creative and desire to see my students again, I know it's time to fix those files and begin a new year!

Chapter 8
Training Itinerant Student Teachers

The Need to Train Itinerants

Graduate courses for student teachers of the deaf and hard of hearing often assume that the teacher will work in a self-contained classroom. As more and more teachers gain itinerant employment to support the increasing number of mainstreamed students with hearing losses, graduate schools of education need to focus more on the special skills required of itinerants, particularly in the areas of consultation, instructional skills, personal organization, and independence.

The consultation and personal organization skills needed by the itinerant are both quantitatively and qualitatively different from those of the self-contained classroom teacher of the deaf and hard of hearing. Quantitatively, the itinerant is usually assigned more students, and so must possess a higher degree of organization to achieve, in the shortest possible time, high-quality interpersonal contacts with a larger array of teachers, parents, school staff, and community resources. Professional training in the quantitative aspects could lean upon the skills of successful outside salespersons, including the maintenance of contact lists, the use of comprehensive planning devices such as the Franklin or Day Timer products, and the fostering of a customer service attitude.

Qualitatively, the itinerant must become skilled in serving a more diverse clientele. Unlike the teacher who works in a single school, the itinerant must be able to move comfortably among the faculty, students, and parents in a number of communities. This is likely to require, for example, skill in working with a greater variety of national and ethnic cultures than one is likely to encounter in a single school. In addition, the successful itinerant must be thoroughly versed in the skills of concise, responsive customer service. In a fast-paced era of emails, faxes, and heightened expectations about quality of service, the successful itinerant will not be satisfied until all her clientele are satisfied.

Instructional skills are a second area of potential difference between the classroom teacher and the itinerant. Because the itinerant has limited time to reinforce what was taught, it may be argued that more advanced instructional skills are required. The old adage of "Do it right the first time, because you may never get a second chance" may apply here. Even the most intensive IEP seldom provides for more than two or three brief contacts with a student weekly, and in the meantime the regular classroom curricula move relentlessly onward. Reinforcement time is a precious commodity. (There is an intriguing field of research here for the specialist in instructional techniques. For example, in the teaching of reading to hard of hearing students, which techniques result in effective learning, *with the minimum investment of time in reinforcement?*)

A final difference is the degree of independence required of itinerants. Obviously every teacher must have a certain degree of independence which is measured every day the teacher enters the classroom without other adult help. But the self-contained classroom teacher of the deaf and hard of hearing has the advantage of working in a single facility supported by the school's nearby staff. While the itinerant teacher can also depend on some support from each school's staff, the realities of moving efficiently from student to student in many schools requires a much higher degree of self-sufficiency.

Sample Guidelines for the Student Teaching Experience

The complete training of a skilled itinerant teacher is, of course, the job of the graduate schools. However, experienced itinerant teachers are becoming increasingly involved. As a culminating experience in their professional training, prospective itinerant teachers are frequently assigned to student teach under the mentorship of a tenured itinerant.

The following is a suggested set of materials that a school district and the mentor itinerant could use in supervising the student teacher over a ten-week period. These materials are an adaptation of those developed in 1995 for student teachers from Lewis and Clark College who were assigned to the Columbia Regional Program for Deaf and hard of hearing. The regional program, administered by Portland Public Schools on behalf of many school districts in northwest Oregon, serves over 500 students, birth to grade 14.

All participants in the training experience—the college supervisor, the mentor itinerant (sometimes called a cooperating teacher or master teacher), and the student teacher—should receive a copy of all the materials. The materials include:

- *Guidelines for Itinerant Student Teaching,* a program outline describing timelines, evaluative expectations, and an introduction of the supervising mentor teacher.

- *Memo from the Mentor Itinerant Teacher,* assigning specific student teaching activities, and describing the support which the student teacher can expect from the mentor. Written in the first person, this memo is designed to be the first step in the development of a close professional relationship between the two.

- *Observation of Itinerant Student Teacher*, used by the mentor teacher to provide same-day feedback to the student teacher on strengths and opportunities for improvement in instructional technique. Also used by the mentor teacher for reference when completing portions of the Evaluation of Itinerant Student Teacher.

- *Evaluation of Itinerant Student Teacher,* used to evaluate the performance of the student teacher at the midpoint and end of the student teaching experience.

Copies of these materials are shown on the following pages.

Guidelines For Itinerant Student Teaching

Welcome to your student teaching with deaf and hard of hearing students! This experience is designed to help you gain the new knowledge and skills you will need to successfully teach deaf and hard of hearing students. Please read and follow the guidelines below.

Time Schedules and Expectations

The student teacher is expected to conform to the time schedule, activities, regulations, and procedures that apply to the mentor itinerant teacher. For example, the student teacher is expected to arrive at the work site at the time the itinerant teacher is required to report, and to leave when the itinerant teacher is permitted to end the work day. The student teacher is expected to take on all the responsibilities, when appropriate, in common with the itinerant teacher. The student teacher is also expected to attend all meetings required of the itinerant teacher, such as regional, program, and school faculty meetings, parent-teacher conferences, and IEP and Transition meetings.

Mentor teachers as well as student teachers often ask, "How soon should the student teacher take over full responsibility for the work load?" The answer to this question will vary, depending upon the student teacher's previous teaching experience, preparation, and readiness. Usually the assumption of responsibility will progress rapidly if the student teacher has had previous classroom teaching experience. In one case, a student teacher with two years' classroom experience was able to take over most work load responsibilities after two weeks, with the itinerant providing fairly light supervision. Another student teacher with no previous teaching experience, however, was not ready to begin assuming responsibilities until later in the term.

Here is a typical schedule that may be altered to meet the developmental needs of the student teacher:

Week 1: Orientation to the district, staff, students, instructional role, schools, curriculum, schedules, rules, procedures, etc.

Week 2: Plan with the mentor teacher the transitions in responsibility from teacher to student teacher. The student teacher may act as tutor and teacher assistant. The student teacher may be ready to assume more responsibility. By now both the student teacher and the mentor teacher should be relating to one another in a more comfortable manner. The student teacher should feel comfortable asking for clarification and other pertinent information.

Week 3: The student teacher is responsible for a portion of the work load. The student teacher plans with the mentor teacher for assuming an additional part of the work load. The student teacher continues to act as a tutor and teacher assistant during the times he or she is not responsible for the work load.

Week 4: The student teacher takes over the majority of the work load responsibilities.

Because the itinerant teacher does not see each student on a daily basis, issues may surface that require the special attention of the more experienced mentor teacher, even after the student teacher has taken on most responsibilities. This may occur because the student teacher has little shared history with the student, whereas the itinerant may have taught some of the assigned students for several years. For example, recently when a student teacher began working with a student, the mentor teacher noticed that the student was in distress. He wasn't able to concentrate on his work. The mentor teacher asked the student teacher to step aside and engaged the student in conversation. The student exclaimed, "Why am I the only one who needs to use an FM? Nobody else has to use hearing aids! Why ME? IT'S NOT FAIR!" This was a critical and difficult moment in this student's development, which the cooperating teacher had been expecting for some time. The teacher spent considerable time exploring with the student his concern about his hearing loss and its ramifications.

The student teacher had a rare opportunity to observe a deaf student developing his self-concept, and how the itinerant helped him through the process. There will be moments like this when, for the good of the student, the cooperating teacher must step in. It is a time for the student teacher to gracefully step back, and use it as an opportunity to learn a teaching technique. Similarly, there may be times when the mentor teacher will need to be the lead professional in a contact with a parent or teacher because of a delicate previous history. This is an opportunity for the student teacher to observe the cooperating teacher's consultation technique, and later discuss the historical context in which the consultation occurred.

Week 5: The student teacher takes over all of the responsibility of the itinerant teacher, if appropriate.

Weeks 6-10: The student teacher continues full responsibility for all aspects of the itinerant teacher's work load where appropriate. As the weeks go by, the itinerant teacher should let the student teacher conduct the responsibilities of the job without close supervision for longer and longer periods of time.

It is important for the itinerant to confer with the student teacher several times a week, to provide feedback on the student teacher's performance, and to guide the student teacher's planning.

Evaluation

The mentor teacher is encouraged to provide the student teacher feedback on a continuous basis, and to evaluate the student teacher formally twice during the ten-week period. Each aspect of the student teacher's performance should be reviewed, including lesson planning, lesson presentation, material and media use, visual representation of concepts being taught, collaboration and consultative skills, communication abilities, and student assessment. The mentor itinerant teacher should also evaluate the student teacher's professional knowledge, behavior, and attitudes.

The first formal evaluation should be completed after the fifth week of the student teaching assignment. The results should be shared with the student teacher and the college supervisor. This evaluation is a progress report that identifies both areas of strength and areas needing improvement.

The final student teaching evaluation is completed at the end of the tenth week. After first being shared with the student teacher, the evaluation should be shared with and given to the college supervisor. If appropriate, a letter of recommendation from the mentor itinerant should be forwarded to the student's college placement file. Finally, the mentor itinerant teacher and the college supervisor will complete and submit any evaluation forms required by the state licensing board.

Memo from the Mentor Itinerant Teacher

Following is a memo that can be used by the mentor teacher to introduce himself/herself to the student teacher.

MEMO

TO: [Name of Student Teacher]

FROM: [Name of Mentor Itinerant Teacher]

DATE: [First Date of Student Teaching Assignment]

SUBJECT: Itinerant Student Teaching

Welcome to your student teaching assignment as an itinerant teacher! I hope you will find this a time of professional growth, and I'm looking forward to the opportunity to help you in that process. I believe you will find, as I have, that an itinerant teacher plays a key role in helping deaf and hard of hearing students succeed in school and their communities.

The guidelines below are intended to help you succeed as an itinerant. Both you and I will use them to assess your learning and growth.

1. Continue Educating Yourself about the Deaf and Hard of Hearing. You will be responsible for developing your knowledge of deaf and hard of hearing culture and issues by proposing a set of experiences that will help you grow professionally. Such activities might include attending specific functions in the deaf community, conversing with deaf and hard of hearing adults, and reading publications regarding deafness. Let's discuss soon. I can brief you on opportunities I know about, and you can describe your interests. Then prepare a schedule of your activities, including checkpoints when we should review what you have learned.

2. Learn about Community Services Available to Parents and Students. You will be responsible for developing a method of demonstrating your knowledge of community services in the geographical area in which you do your student teaching. This could be a written report, an assembled file of brochures from agencies that provide relevant services, or some other method. Let's discuss how you'd like to do this. You may want to incorporate your activities on this project into the same schedule as described above in Item 1.

3. Keep a Daily Journal. Before each day ends, record your key experiences in a journal. This could be in a Franklin Planner, a Day Timer, or some similar planner. Describe concisely what you did, what you learned, and what you might do differently in the future. Because each day of itinerant teaching is different from the one before it, your journal will help you gain insight into an itinerant's work by reflecting on each day while it is still fresh in your mind. Let's use this as a discussion starter at least once a week.

4. Keep a Dialogue Journal with Me. You will be traveling with me daily, and we'll be talking together as we make our rounds. In addition, (if you and I agree that this would be a helpful strategy) keeping a written dialogue journal with questions and insights for us to discuss will help you explore a different method of communication. For example, if you are watching me teach a student and you don't understand why I use a particular technique, write your question down right away. Later, I'll write my answer. This is also a method that you will be able to use profitably with your future students.

5. Student Profiles. An itinerant teacher must keep documentation on all students served. As part of your experience, you will need to assemble information on each student who is included in your caseload. This includes a) samples of the student's work; b) any test results; c) the student's audiogram; d) the student's IEP; e) any other language, speech, reading, and writing goals not in the student's IEP; and f) anything else pertaining to the student. Your college supervisor will probably have suggestions, and may require you to write an in-depth assessment of a particular student.

The requirement for learning goals outside of the IEP may seem incongruous. How could a student have language goals not listed in the annual IEP? Frequently that's the case. For example, the classroom teacher may tell the itinerant that the student is having a difficult time understanding a particular concept related to an earlier   lesson. Now is the time to clarify that concept for the student even though it is not expressly mentioned in the IEP goals. Or maybe the student is having difficulties with other children at recess. This is the teachable moment: help the student clarify the nature of the conflict and decide what to do. If the itinerant has established a trustful relationship with each student, it will be easier and quicker to deal with such issues as they arise, even though they are not in the IEP.

6. The Matter of Lesson Plans. If this were a self-contained classroom experience, you would be preparing daily lesson plans. However, for your direct serve students, you will be supporting the lesson plans of the regular classroom teacher as well as the IEP goals. So if the teacher hasn't briefed you in advance but wants your help, his/her lesson plan is the first thing you find out about when you enter the classroom. At other times the teacher will ask the itinerant to teach or reinforce a skill previously taught or missing from the student's knowledge bank. And while it is important for the itinerant to make tentative instructional plans for each meeting with a student, frequently those plans must be postponed to fill the requests of the classroom teacher.

While all this may be potentially frustrating and ambiguous, the good news is that the itinerant does less daily lesson planning than most teachers; today's plan for a direct serve student may not be used until later in the week. The bad news—at least for those who like to be in high control of their lives—is that you must be able to react quickly to where the instruction is right now, as you enter the classroom. It is the student's success in the classroom which is primary, not the convenience of the itinerant's planning.

In some cases, however, direct serve students are instructed by you outside the regular classroom and its curriculum. You will be expected to prepare and use your own lesson plan for each of these meetings. The lesson plan format that you have learned in your earlier graduate work can be used with your direct serve students; there is no required district "form." Your plans should be thorough and precise, and include instructional objectives, materials, procedures, and an evaluation component. They should be detailed enough so that a substitute could carry them out. As you begin to take on instructional responsibility for your direct serve students, I will periodically review your plans and provide feedback.

Consult students do not require lesson plans. Your relationship here is one of monitoring the progress of the student, checking the student's assistive devices, and providing guidance to the teacher, staff, and parents.

7. Assessments. Another experience you will have this term is participating in student assessments. Our time with each student is so short that often we don't have time for written pre- and post-assessments. But nonwritten assessment of skills and knowledge does occur daily, and this is a skill I want you to observe and learn. Watch me and let's include this in our dialogue as we move from school to school.

However, when we are preparing for a student's IEP, staffing, three-year evaluation, transition, or other structured meeting with parents or staff, we may sometimes be asked to prepare written assessments of the student's skills and knowledge. I will ask you to take the lead role in preparing some of these assessments.

8. Keep a Contact Log. Itinerant teachers are required to account for their time, so that service rendered in support of IEPs can be proven and reported. Your written documentation of *all* contacts and services will be used to keep track of consultation time, academic lessons taught, hearing aids checked, and any other related services. Periodically you and I will compare our documentation to see how close our records match.

Documentation of an instructional lesson may be as brief as a single sentence entry; it is not detailed like a lesson plan. Be sure that you have a clear objective in mind if you veer from your plan, and use the contact log to record what you have taught and why. This information will help you clarify to the staff, parents, student, college supervisor, and your mentor teacher the reasons behind your decisions. You will be surprised how many times you will refer to this documentation, especially if legal issues arise in relation to a particular student.

9. Final Project. For your final project you will be asked to write a paper reflecting on your student teaching experience. Some of the things you may want to include are your observations of others' consultation and instruction, and summaries of what you did, what you learned, and how you see yourself including some of these things into your future teaching career. You may add any other items that are of value to you.

10. Student Teaching Notebook. All of the above work is to be organized into a student teaching notebook, sometimes called a portfolio. Before you start your student teaching experience, decide how you will collect your data, so that you won't be burdened with a multitude of activity calendars, journals, and the like. Remember, the successful itinerant travels efficiently! Let's discuss data collection before you start any of the above projects. I'd like to share with you how I keep my records. The quicker we handle record keeping, the more students, teachers and parents we can serve!

Attached to this memo are the observation and evaluation forms we'll be using.

Observation of Itinerant Student Teacher

Student Teacher _____ Date _____

Activity Observed _____

Directions: Based on performance that can reasonably be expected of a student teacher, please rate the performance of this individual from 1 (low) to 5 (high), with 3 indicating average performance. Write N/O if this aspect was not observed, and N/A if it is not applicable to the activity being observed.

Performance Observed	Rating	Comments, as Needed
Planning:		
Clear objectives		
Uses appropriate methods		
Uses appropriate materials		
Uses assistive listening devices		
Structure of Lesson:		
Opening		
Maintains rapport		
Secures student attention		
Reviews rules/expectations		
States goal/purpose		
Reviews relevant preskills		
Body of Lesson		
Demonstrates		
Explains procedures		
Prompts student		
Fades prompts		
Monitors independent work		
Close		
Reviews lesson taught		
Introduces independent work		
Transitions to next activity		
Collects data		
Uses data for lesson planning		

	Rating	Comments, as Needed

Presentation Skills:

	Rating	Comments
Uses appropriate communication system		
Teaches to student's language level		
Speaks and signs clearly		
Understands student's language		
Uses visually based instruction		
Adapts curriculum materials		
Keeps student's attention		
Elicits responses		
Maintains appropriate pace		
Provides equal response opportunities		
Maximizes success (80-90%)		
Gives appropriate feedback		

Professional Skills:

	Rating	Comments
Verbal communication		
Nonverbal communication		
Rapport with staff		
Knowledge of interpreter role		
Ability to work with interpreter/assistant		
Spelling		
Handwriting		

Summary of Strengths:

Selected Objectives for Improvement:

Cooperating Teacher _____ Date _____

Student Teacher _____ Date _____

Evaluation of Itinerant Student Teacher

Student Teacher _____ Term/Year _____

School districts served _____

Schools served _____

Grades or age levels taught _____ Subjects taught _____

Cooperating Teacher _____ College Supervisor _____

Directions: Based on performance that can reasonably be expected of a student teacher, please rate the performance of this individual from 1 (low) to 5 (high), with 3 indicating average performance. Write N/O if this aspect was not observed, and N/A if it is not applicable to the teaching role being evaluated.

Performance Characteristic	Rating	Comments, as Needed
1. Hearing Issues Awareness. Continues to learn about the deaf and hard of hearing culture, related issues, and community services available for persons with hearing losses.		
2. Data Collection. Collects data relevant for student direct service and consultation through the use of a daily journal, dialogue journal, student profiles, student assessments, and contact log.		
3. Assessment. Uses appropriate strategies for assessing the student's knowledge and skill in language, speech, literacy, behavior, and communicative competence.		

	Rating	Comments, as Needed
4. Planning. Develops appropriate lesson plans and teaching sequences with appropriate objectives and goals.		
5. Instructional Delivery. Can transfer goals and objectives from the IEP, using diverse teaching strategies appropriate to the concepts and skills being taught. Modifies activities for individual differences, age appropriateness, and learning styles; uses questions to promote higher order thinking; and fosters each student's language development.		
6. Use of Instructional Space and Time. Arranges the classroom, or other teaching space, to optimize learning. Uses instructional time efficiently, including consistent involvement of students in learning activities.		
7. Reinforcement. Provides students with effective feedback, encourages students to be active learners, and consistently uses materials to visually represent and reinforce information.		
8. Behavior Management. Consistently employs effective behavior management techniques.		
9. Student Evaluation. Keeps accurate data regarding student progress, and uses this information to modify instruction.		

	Rating	Comments, as Needed
10. Team Member. Is able to work and collaborate effectively as a team member with the mentor teacher.		
11. Consulting Activities. Is able to consult effectively with classroom teachers, parents, administrators, interpreters, and students.		
12. Materials Support. Provides teachers and students with appropriate level material to enhance the learning process.		
13. Special Services Coordination. Coordinates special services which the student may need from teachers, other school staff, parents, and the community.		
14. Alertness to Emerging Problems. Is alert to social, emotional, environmental, and other possible problems the student may have. Knows when a team meeting or referral is appropriate.		
15. Communication. Communicates effectively with students, parents, and school staff.		
16. Self-Evaluation. Realistically evaluates own teaching performance, is open to suggestions and criticism, and uses mentor teacher's feedback to improve teaching performance. Responds insightfully to student teaching experiences (what I did, what I learned, observations, and reflections) as demonstrated in a written paper.		

	Rating	Comments, as Needed
17. Professionalism. Demonstrates knowledge of subject matter, methodology, educational issues, theories, and materials. Does work promptly, independently, and thoroughly. Works effectively with others, is flexible, uses common sense, and exhibits confidence. Demonstrates positive interactions with students, teachers, parents, and administrators.		

COMMENTS: On an attached blank sheet of paper, if needed, expand on the ratings, discuss general attributes, or assess personal qualities or instructional skills.

Cooperating Teacher: _____ Date _____

Alternative Evaluation Forms

For the mentor itinerant teacher desiring an approach that sets predetermined learning objectives and relates those objectives to curricular goals, the following Student Teaching Evaluation by Objective may be more helpful than the form shown immediately above. The Student Teaching Evaluation by Objective was initially developed at Western Oregon State College and has been adapted by the author for use with itinerant student teachers of the deaf and hard of hearing.

A second alternative evaluation form, Final Evaluation of Itinerant Student Teacher, appears at the end of this chapter. It also has been adapted by the author from a Western Oregon State College form. This form has the largest number of rating categories.

So which of the evaluation forms is best? Whichever best reflects your style of teaching, the needs of the student teacher, and the requirements of the program in which you work. The form is merely a tool to describe the degree of success your student teacher has had in your learning environment. And if none of the forms seems "best," perhaps parts of them suggest what your own personalized form might be.

Student Teacher Evaluation by Objective

Student Teacher _____ Term/Year _____

School districts served _____

Schools served _____

Grades or age levels taught _____ Subjects taught _____

Mentor Teacher _____ College Supervisor _____

Student Teaching Goals

Goal 1. To assess, diagnose, and evaluate learners.

Goal 2. To plan and implement instructional plans, using suitable curriculum methods.

Goal 3. To be able to implement appropriate management techniques, utilizing effective educational intervention.

Goal 4. To gradually assume management of all phases of an itinerant teacher's role and assignments that are appropriate.

Goal 5. If appropriate, to collaborate with classroom teachers of mainstreamed students.

Instructions

The following is a list of objectives that have been identified to meet the goals of student teaching listed on the previous page. The student teacher should attach examples of activities that demonstrate completion of these objectives. The mentor teacher may add comments. Each activity and comment should be coded with the same number as its related objective.

The mentor teacher should rate the student teacher on each objective using the following rating scale:

5: Excellent; 4: Above Average; 3: Satisfactory; 2: Below Average;
1: Unsatisfactory; NA: Not Applicable

Goal 1: To assess, diagnose, and evaluate learners.	Rating					
	1	2	3	4	5	NA
1.1 The student teacher will demonstrate knowledge of the site special education procedures, i.e., preferral, referral, eligibility.						
1.2 The student teacher will administer and score locally developed and commercially available tests according to their manuals' direction.						
1.3 The student teacher will administer and score a teacher-prepared pre/post assessment.						
1.4 The student teacher will pinpoint maladaptive behaviors when assessing students' behavior needs.						

1.5

The student teacher will review one student's complete assessment results (cognitive, academic, behavior, medical).

1.6

The student teacher will sit in on one student's multidisciplinary team meeting.

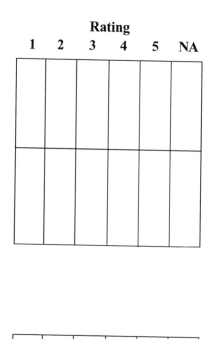

Goal 2: To plan and implement instructional plans, using suitable curriculum methods.

2.1

The student teacher will become familiar with the site IEP forms.

2.2

The student teacher will observe/ participate in the IEP process. The process should include meeting with parents and school personnel.

2.3

Given a set of assessment results, the student teacher will develop long- and-short term behavioral objectives to include academic, behavioral, and transition areas.

2.4

The student teacher will develop two instructional programs clearly related to written learning goals (Work Samples).

	1	2	3	4	5	NA

2.5
The student teacher will implement instructional plans using various teaching methods (including AV equipment/media, strategies, and techniques) to achieve planned objectives (Work Samples).

2.6
The student teacher will select/use a variety of formal and informal means of assessment to determine student achievement (Work Samples).

2.7
The student teacher will establish a climate conducive to learning by communicating rules, monitoring student conduct, providing meaningful reinforcement, setting up materials in advance of teaching, and coordinating the use of instructional assistants.

Goal 3: To be able to implement appropriate management techniques, utilizing effective educational intervention.

3.1
The student teacher will manage student behaviors in an instructional setting.

3.2
The student teacher will manage student behavior during transitional and non-instructional time.

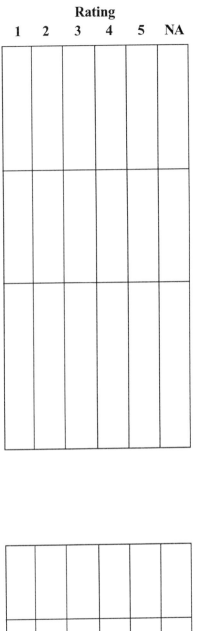

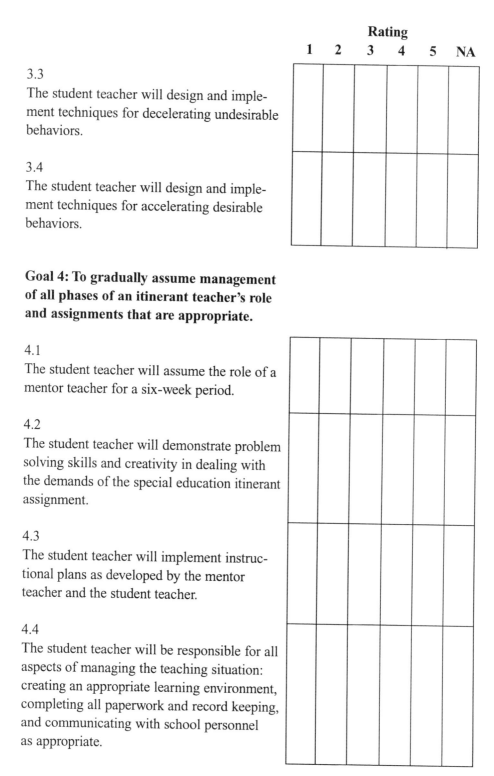

3.3
The student teacher will design and implement techniques for decelerating undesirable behaviors.

3.4
The student teacher will design and implement techniques for accelerating desirable behaviors.

Goal 4: To gradually assume management of all phases of an itinerant teacher's role and assignments that are appropriate.

4.1
The student teacher will assume the role of a mentor teacher for a six-week period.

4.2
The student teacher will demonstrate problem solving skills and creativity in dealing with the demands of the special education itinerant assignment.

4.3
The student teacher will implement instructional plans as developed by the mentor teacher and the student teacher.

4.4
The student teacher will be responsible for all aspects of managing the teaching situation: creating an appropriate learning environment, completing all paperwork and record keeping, and communicating with school personnel as appropriate.

	Rating					
	1	2	3	4	5	NA

4.5
The student teacher will demonstrate a high level of professionalism at all times, e.g., punctuality, tact, composure.

Goal 5: If appropriate, to collaborate with classroom teachers of mainstreamed students.

5.1
The student teacher will demonstrate the ability to assist classroom teachers in adjusting curriculum for deaf and hard of hearing students in the regular classroom appropriate to student IEP goals and objectives.

5.2
The student teacher will demonstrate the ability to work effectively with interpreters, real time captioners, instructional assistants, and peer tutors.

5.3
The student teacher will demonstrate the ability to coordinate support services and personnel schedules to meet individual student needs and IEP goals and objectives.

Mentor Itinerant Teacher _____ Date _____

69

Final Evaluation of Itinerant Student Teacher

Student Teacher _____ Term/Year _____

School districts served _____

Schools served _____

Grades or age levels taught _____ Subjects taught _____

Mentor Teacher _____ College Supervisor _____

Directions. Please check the appropriate boxes, using the rating scale. Attach any comments you may wish to make.

Ratings: 5: Excellent; 4: Above Average; 3: Satisfactory;
             2: Below Average; 1: Unsatisfactory; NA: Not Applicable

Personal Characteristics:

	Rating					
	1	2	3	4	5	NA
1. **Personal Traits.** Tact; patience; consideration; emotional control; temperament; freedom from mannerisms; general mental health; general attitude; sense of humor						
2. **Character.** Honesty; fairness; sincerity; tolerance; maturity; promptness; perseverance; reliability; initiative; independence; industry; ability to accept responsibility						
3. **Appearance.** Neatness; grooming; posture; appropriate dress; poise						
4. **Expressive Communication.** Accuracy and clarity of signs and fingerspelling; consistent use of oral and/or manual components (as appropriate)						

70

	1	2	3	4	5	NA

5. **Receptive Communication.**
   Understanding expressive communication, signed and/or orally produced by students

6. **Language.** Correctness, clarity of expression, vocabulary in American Sign Language (ASL), oral English, written English, ability to use language and vocabulary appropriate to the child's age and development, handwriting, spelling, fingerspelling

7. **Mental Traits.** Good judgment, open-mindedness, intellectual honesty, curiosity, logic of thought, critical ability, ability to accept criticism and profit from it

8. **Cooperation.** Relationships with mentor teacher, school personnel, parents, students

Instructional Teaching Characteristics:

9. **Knowledge of Subject**

   a. Knowledge of language development at the level taught

   b. Knowledge of academic areas appropriate to that level (arithmetic, social studies, science, etc.)

   c. Integrated subject matter with ASL and/or English language and communication skills

   d. Accuracy of all information taught

	1	2	3	4	5	NA
e. Understands interrelationships between various areas of knowledge						

10. Planning Learning Activities

   a. Selects objectives appropriate to the needs of the student/group and the material being presented

   b. States these objectives clearly

   c. Plans the means for determining the extent to which the objectives have been accomplished

   d. Meets the requirements of the mentor teacher regarding lesson plans

11. Teaching Techniques

   a. Selects learning experiences appropriate to objectives

   b. Organizes and properly sequences learning experiences

   c. Uses a variety of procedures

   d. Foresees and plans the resolution of possible difficulties that might be encountered

   e. Evaluates his/her own teaching objectively

12. Presentation

   a. Motivates, stimulates, and holds the interest of the student

	1	2	3	4	5	NA
b. Presents a lesson in an organized, sequential order						
c. Utilizes time so that the maximum amount of learning is accomplished in the minimum amount of time						
d. Recognizes individual interests, levels of learning, and needs within the group and provides adequately for these differences						
e. Maintains flexibility while teaching in terms of pacing, lesson time, content, etc.						
f. Takes advantage of incidents that occur unexpectedly and utilizes them in providing worthwhile learning experiences						
g. Adjusts communication with hard of hearing or deaf children to their level of language development and sentence structure						

13. *Skill in the teaching environment*

	1	2	3	4	5	NA
a. Analyzes types of errors made by students and revises plans to correct these learning difficulties						
b. Leads the students to discovery and independent thinking through skillful questioning on their level						
c. Develops responsibility on the part of the students to use their best language and communication skills at all times						

	1	2	3	4	5	NA

   d. Keeps all students constructively
      involved throughout the class period

14. *Environmental Management*

   a. Keeps environment orderly, attractive,
      and as physically comfortable
      as possible

   b. Gives instruction in and holds
      students responsible for proper care
      and use of books, supplies, and
      amplification equipment

   c. Keeps all records up to date, including
      samples of each student's work
      showing his/her progress

   d. Is well prepared for the day's work
      before teaching and makes good use
      of planning time

   e. Maintains control and encourages
      appropriate student conduct

15. *Understanding of Student*

   a. Develops good personal relationships
      with students

   b. Is aware of the ability and progress of
      each student in the group

   c. Is fair and objective at all times in
      dealing with students

   d. Gains the confidence and respect of
      students

	1	2	3	4	5	NA
e. Shows insight into child behavior						

16. *Teaching Materials*

	1	2	3	4	5	NA
a. Selects suitable teaching materials for the level taught						
b. Adapts materials when those available are not wholly suitable						
c. Shows creativity and originality in developing teacher-made materials to fill all gaps						
d. Makes effective use of all teaching materials, audiovisual aids, and equipment						

Consultant Characteristics

	1	2	3	4	5	NA
17. Assists classroom teacher in adapting lessons for deaf and hard of hearing students						
18. Demonstrates awareness of regular education curriculum and program						
19. Shows flexibility in dealing with different teacher styles and in scheduling/planning						
20. Displays good consultation skills (team member, active listening, problem-solving)						
21. Uses hearing-aid analyzer, FMs and other assistive devices with ease						

	1	2	3	4	5	NA
22. Recognizes and attends to cultural needs of deaf and hard of hearing students in the mainstream (books, assemblies, field trips)						

Professional Characteristics

23. *Attitudes Toward Teaching.* Interest in teaching as a profession, initiative and enthusiasm in professional activities, professional discretion, reliability and loyalty						
24. *Ability to Work with Others.* Desire and ability to establish satisfactory personal and professional relationships with school personnel, as well as with students and parents						
25. *Participation in Co-Curricular Activities*						
26. *Probable Success as a Teacher*						

Suggested Grade_____

Mentor Teacher_____ Date _____

Chapter 9

On the Road in East County

Previous chapters have described methods and techniques for the itinerant teacher. But what's it really like to be an itinerant? Come along with me on a recent week. The events are real; only the names of persons and schools have been changed.

Monday, 7:30 a.m. The morning's first sound is the electronic voice of my message phone. "You have no messages," it announces with a dull impersonality which reflects the gray drizzle outside. Good. That will give me time for breakfast. Then I finish packing my car with the usual array of teaching materials, and leave our suburban home. Turning north on the interstate, I thread my way through the damp morning commute toward my first student of the day.

8:40 a.m. Amber is a well-designed middle school which was once spacious, but now struggles to accommodate its growing student population as apartments begin to replace the community's older single-family homes. I meet Carlos in the nurse's office, the best space available. He is a fast-growing, bilingual Latino, faced with multiple disabilities: vision, mental retardation, and moderate to severe hearing loss in both ears. We work together on reading and writing skills. We have far to go. Although Carlos is mainstreamed in the eighth grade, he is only reading at second grade level. Fortunately, he has been assigned a full time aide. I think he will complete school, but his retardation will always require him to live with his parents or in a supervised group home.

9:20 a.m. I leave Amber and drive six miles east. Traffic is lighter now, and we're getting a few hopeful sun breaks as I pull into the parking lot of Longfellow Grade School. With wild abandon, I risk leaving my umbrella in the car and slip inside to the psychologist's office. The psychologist isn't in on Mondays, so it makes a fine place to meet Michelle. Strongwilled and apparently rather uncommunicative by nature, Michelle is battling her way through fifth grade with mixed results. She struggles with learning disabilities and a unilateral, severe hearing loss. Sometimes children with a loss in one ear only don't instinctively learn well, and that seems true for Michelle. We work together on social studies concepts and related vocabulary. Michelle reads well orally, but doesn't comprehend much of what she reads because of low vocabulary skills.

10:15 a.m. I'm running a few minutes late, but I always walk my kids back to the classroom. It's a good time to visit. I am surprised to hear Michelle volunteer that she thinks the tutoring is helping her. Then it's a two mile drive to Hughes Grade School.

10:30 a.m. Mrs. Bailey is the archetypal school secretary who always smiles and remembers everyone's name. She hands me the key to a bare little room where I meet twice a week with Sherry, a second grader. She appears almost immediately in the doorway, full of smiles and energy. She has a profound unilateral hearing loss. The multidisciplinary team (MDT) is concerned about her reading progress, so I am helping her in reading and writing. Today we work on beginning consonant sounds and short vowel sounds. I am impressed at how persistently Sherry responds to my instruction, even though she's not particularly successful. In spite of her constancy, I am beginning to understand her learning disability in addition to her hearing impairment. Sherry needs to experience more success before her happy attitude toward learning erodes.

11:00 a.m. Time for an early lunch. I have 40 minutes until my next student. I leisurely drive six miles west on Bixby Road to Armstrong High School. While I'm driving I sip on my water bottle and munch a granola bar. I stop at my favorite gas station to fill up. Here in Oregon the attendants still do the honors, a welcome service for a rainy climate. Jim is always cheerful, and I enjoy exchanging pleasantries with him. I know from earlier conversations that he has a slight hearing loss. As he begins filling the tank, Jim tells me he had his 25th birthday over the weekend. When my tank is full I continue toward Armstrong High School.

11:20 a.m. Parked in the high school lot, this is my time to listen to the radio, eat lunch, do paperwork, and think about the students I've seen this morning. I feel confident Carlos will find a niche in society, although a limited one. Michelle's response today was warmer than it has ever been. If she believes the tutoring is helping, then maybe we can make some real progress. But, spooning through my plastic container of cottage cheese and pineapple, I become less optimistic as I think of Sherry. Sherry is so oblivious to the inconsistencies in her learning! It is only a matter of time before self-reflection and discouragement set in. I can't seem to get a handle on the unusual twists in her learning style, and I'm glad her speech pathologist has already referred her for a learning disability study. If our team can figure her out, Sherry will have a chance at preserving her happy outlook on learning.

11:40 a.m. David is absent again. My long walk across the soggy campus to his combined social studies and English class has been fruitless. I drop into the counseling office and talk with Karen, David's counselor. Karen is concerned about his mounting absences. We decide that I will talk to David's mother tonight, and then develop a remedial strategy tomorrow.

11:50 a.m. Unexpected free time. Since I'm usually in class for 80 minutes with David, I now have over two hours until my next appointment. So I drive toward my next appointment, and park among some beautiful firs and cedars and switch on the classical station. How peaceful it is here. Not warm enough outside to open the windows yet, but the sun is shining! I pull out the annual Gallaudet University survey of deafness, and begin recording information on each of my twenty-three students. It takes some time to complete the detailed questions about each student's type of deafness and services being received. Finished with that, I turn to my monthly class list and verify current student information.

2:00 p.m. At Vista High School I meet with Matt's English teacher, Mrs. Wall, during her conference period. Matt has a bilateral, profound sensory neural hearing loss, but is doing remarkably well in high school. Instead of a sign language interpreter, he is assigned a real time captioner. The captioner inputs classroom discussion to a modified version of a steno machine, like that used by court reporters. However, the machine's output immediately appears in English on Matt's laptop computer screen. This allows Matt to read, in real time, what is being said. At first, Mrs. Wall and I discuss Matt's grades in preparation for his annual IEP tomorrow, then the conversation begins to expand. She has questions about hearing loss. Nothing particular, only she has time to visit and she wants to understand the world of a deaf student better. The extra time I spend with her today will help her feel more comfortable working with Matt and other deaf students in the future.

3:30 p.m. I'm tired! It's been a full day and it's time to head for home. I like the days that end in Vista because I can drive home through farmland.

4:15 p.m. I check my voice mail. No new messages.

7:10 p.m. Ellen's hesitant voice carries the burden of her worry about David. Because I stay in regular touch with my parents, Ellen and I have no difficulty establishing rapport on the phone. Now in her mid-thirties, Ellen is a single parent struggling to keep herself and her two children together on a low wage. She works a 5:30 a.m. to 2:30 p.m. shift so she can be home at the end of the school day. She shares that David has a different excuse every day for missing school, but the problem seems deeper. He keeps saying he wishes he were dead.

* * * * *

Tuesday, 7:20 a.m. Voice mail message #1 notifies me that Jamal's aid is fixed and ready to be picked up. Message #2 is from an itinerant teacher with information about a social get-together for all our elementary kids. The third message has been left by our audiologist, Jean, wanting more information on my new student, Bobby.

7:30 a.m. I pack the car and head out for science class with David. It's a bad commute.

8:10 a.m. David is absent again! Time to huddle with Karen.

8:20 a.m. I fill Karen in on Ellen's description of David's behavior at home, including the death wish. Karen suggests that maybe he is clinically depressed. We decide I will pass that on to Ellen so she can get it checked out. Also, Karen will convene a staffing with all of his teachers for Friday morning. I'm worried about David. Perhaps the recent events in his life have caused depression. A few months ago the doctor told him to quit junior varsity basketball because of weak knees, and then more recently his parents split.

8:40 a.m. I leave Armstrong High School and drive four miles to Midway Primary School to meet Bobby, a new student at the school, but his class has gone to PE. It's his teacher's prep time, so we discuss Bobby's needs. She agrees that he needs amplification. He is a charming first grader. It will be my job to collect all the paperwork and get him fitted with hearing aids. I'm scheduled to meet him two times a week, and I look forward to bonding with him.

9:15 a.m. Another of my students, Robert, a consult, is in the same school. Robert is an extensively disabled student who spends most of his time sleeping because of seizure medicine which he must take. He owns hearing aids, but because of his mental retardation and other medical disabilities, it is very difficult to estimate the aids' effectiveness. Most of the time he doesn't wear his aids because the teacher doesn't see any difference in his communication or responsiveness. I really wanted to get his current address, but his teacher is out for the day so I'll stop again next week.

9:30 a.m. I walk to the other side of the building and pick up Jacob, a second grader. We walk to the supply room where we work together for 30 minutes. Today we read a story about insects and ladybugs. In spite of his moderate to severe hearing loss, Jacob is doing well in his reading but needs some help with writing skills.

10:00 a.m. I walk Jacob back to his classroom and return down the hall to pick up my third grader, Ivan. English is Ivan's second language, Russian his first, and he has a bilateral, mild to moderate hearing loss. He refuses to wear his hearing aids, and his parents are letting him make that decision. Nevertheless, Ivan is making adequate progress. Today we work on writing sentences using his spelling words from class. Writing sentences is sometimes difficult for him. More importantly, he needs our time together to talk about his feelings and difficulties. He really seems to enjoy our scheduled time together.

10:45 a.m. After walking Ivan back to his classroom, I meet my new first grader, Bobby. We get acquainted and talk about his hearing. I do some informal assessments of his learning. I am surprised that someone hasn't discovered his hearing loss before this time. But at least he's going to get the help he needs in the near future. I call our audiologist and order an FM for Bobby to use at school until he gets hearing aids. Then I drive to the regional hearing program offices.

Noon. I pick up Jamal's aid at the audiology office, and walk upstairs to the itinerant office. Several other itinerants are there, so we visit and catch up on current news. This time of visiting helps me feel connected to others who share my special kind of work. Today the talk is all about the impending split of our regional special education program into two regions. There will be layoffs from our staff, but the hope is that the new region will hire our layoffees.

12:45 p.m. I process a week's worth of mail—it's been that long since I've been in the office. I draft an upcoming IEP, check the file on a new student who's been referred for service, and call a parent. I start to call Ellen, but then remember that she isn't home from work until later.

2:15 p.m. I arrive at the Special Education office at Vista High School, only to find that the case manager hasn't prepared any of the paperwork for our IEP meeting on Matt. She asks me to run the meeting because she doesn't know him as well as I. Fortunately I have prepared my portion of the paperwork so I can step in for her. Matt is a senior and will be going to college next year, so we focus on transition issues. The formal part of the meeting lasts only a half hour, after which the case manager, the counselor, and the teachers leave. The real time captioner and I linger on with Matt and his parents for another hour to discuss his parents' concerns about the remainder of this year, his summer plans, and college next year. Matt's parents, who have done a wonderful job of guiding Matt's academic career, will be facing different demands and issues as Matt begins to move out into the broader world.

4:00 p.m. We say our good-byes, and I head for home.

7:30 p.m. I tell Ellen that Karen believes David should be checked out by a doctor for severe depression. She agrees to call her HMO the next day for an appointment.

* * * * *

Wednesday, 8:40 a.m. My first student today is Carlos at Amber Middle School. We continue to work on reading and writing skills. As he gains skill, he is becoming more interested and excited about reading and writing. He enjoys working past our allotted time, so I stay with him as long as my schedule permits.

9:30 a.m. Time to send Carlos back to class and drive over to Hughes Grade School.

10:00 a.m. Parked at Hughes, I catch up on my student contact report for 15 minutes, then go into the school to update Sherry's case manager on my suspicion that Sherry has a learning disability. I make a note to complete my portion of the IEP and submit the appropriate paperwork.

10:30 a.m. Sherry and I work on writing a story about a fictitious "Terrible Horrible Bad Day" that she had. Her teacher will be typing each of the student stories for their books. Sherry understands exactly what needs to be done, so we have a productive half hour.

11:00 a.m. Time's up with Sherry. I drive to Armstrong High School, turn on some music, and quietly eat my lunch in the parking lot. These moments are important because I have time just to meditate, without any demands being put on me.

11:45 a.m. David is absent again! I'll be glad when he comes back. After teaching him for four years, I'm missing his sparkling smile and our time together. At 6'4", he towers over me when we walk down the hallway. I'm concerned about him.

12:05 p.m. After visiting briefly with Karen, I drive to Running Creek Elementary School. Mrs. Erickson, who has a special education classroom, wants me to observe one of her girls, because she has noticed what she thinks is a sudden hearing loss.

12:15 p.m. The girl I'm supposed to observe is absent, so Mrs. Erickson and I discuss her observations and concerns. I will call the parent of the girl and discuss the matter with her. Making cold calls to teachers and parents is always a difficult thing for me to do, but the phone visit with the mom flows smoothly.

1:00 p.m. I leave Running Creek and return to Amber Middle School. When I was there in the morning, I had confirmed that Sara, a chronic absentee without parental support, was present. However, now a teacher tells me he saw her leave campus at lunchtime with a boy, and she hasn't returned yet. She and I are supposed to work together for an 80-minute period two or three times a week, but we are lucky to average once a week. Only an eighth grader, Sara is on her way to becoming a dropout. Even though the staff and I are trying to help her turn her life around, I suspect we will fail. She has so much potential! It's hard to be a teacher when you have to watch, powerless, as a life deteriorates.

1:45 p.m. I make a series of phone calls to confirm arrangements for a project I am working on with four other itinerant teachers. We will be doing a presentation to the rest of our staff in May on current technology for deaf and hard of hearing students. My part is real time captioning technology.

4:30 p.m. Ellen calls to share with me how worried she is about David. He continues to slide further into his depression. He is repeating that he doesn't want to live. David's appointment with the doctor isn't until Friday afternoon. He has decided not to go to school until next week. My heart goes out to him. Life in the hearing world is so difficult for deaf and hard of hearing kids, and to have clinical depression besides must feel overwhelming. Still, I suspect David will overcome this dark period. I'll keep him and his mom in my prayers. It's both a gift and a burden to be so trusted, so involved with my parents and students.

* * * * *

Thursday, 8:30 a.m. David is absent again today so I drive to our office. There I turn in Matt's IEP, my Deaf Survey, and my January Class List. I check my mail box, copy a workbook I want to use with Bobby, and get back on the road to Midway Primary School.

9:30 a.m. Jacob and I work on planning a story. We need to plot it out before writing it in his book. He decides to write about a boy named Jeff and his friends who always sing the "ABC Song."

10:00 a.m. After I walk Jacob back to his classroom, I spend a few minutes updating my student contacts into my planner. Then I pick up Ivan from his third grade classroom.

10:15 a.m. Ivan is struggling with writing his thoughts down in logical sentences. So today we are answering some written questions from his teacher about the story his reading group read today. He also struggles with concentration, so we have chosen to work at a table in the hall, rather than the supply room, so he can practice choosing to concentrate on his work rather than the distractions of the hallway.

10:45 a.m. After walking Ivan back to his classroom I pick up Bobby. We're still getting acquainted. He's looking forward to using the FM system which has arrived. We begin today by learning some of the Dolche Sight Vocabulary Words. Then we write those words in the story book I made for him.

11:15 a.m. I return Bobby to his room and drive to Kimberly Middle School.

11:30 a.m. I lug the heavy Fonix Box System into the middle school and check both of Connie's aids. Her right aid is working properly, but her left aid cuts in and out and has lots of static. I carry a first aid tool kit for hearing aids, but there appears to be nothing I can do. Connie wants to keep it for the weekend, so I'll pick it up on Monday and take it to the audiologist.

12:15 p.m. Back at Amber, I eat my lunch and read while listening to some quiet music. An article about mildly hard of hearing kids catches my attention. The author addresses the same questions teachers ask me about hearing impaired students. I make a note in my planner to copy and use the article when I'm orienting my new teachers next year.

1:40 p.m. Walking across campus, I wonder if Sara will be here today. I'm in luck! We find a quiet place and begin working our way through the pile of work she didn't get done while she was absent. Sara is a very open person, and frequently digresses from the lesson at hand to share much of her personal life. Born in Romania, a fall early in life caused her hearing impairment. After arriving in the United States, her life was marred by a number of family tragedies, yet she maintains a surprisingly hopeful outlook on life. The 80 minutes pass quickly.

3:00 p.m. I have only three parents to call. Matt's mom tells me that he's being courted by a prominent midwestern university for track and field. Since he is already nationally ranked in his event, financial aid appears likely. Next I check in with Jamal's mom to find out how he's doing, and whether he's using his aids consistently at home. When I ring Ellen, there is no answer.

7:00 p.m. I reach Ellen. No change with David. We spend most of the time sharing our feelings with each other.

* * * * *

Friday, 7:40 a.m. Six of David's eight teachers, his counselor, his case manager, and I meet to discuss ways of helping David get through this difficult time. We decide that all the teachers will give the work he has missed during the past ten days to his study skills teacher so he won't feel overwhelmed. That teacher will guide David through the work to be made up. His counselor will talk to the athletic director so that, even though he missed the first week of practice, he can still participate in track. An educational aide will help him in math class, his language arts teacher has agreed to a peer helper (whom I will train) on the days I am not with him in class, and I will be with him for each science class and some of the language classes. I really think David will do well enough so he won't have to graduate with a modified diploma. The meeting is over in 20 minutes, and all of the teachers rush off to first period, while I discuss follow-up work with the case manager. I am proud to have been part of an MDT that works the way it was designed. It has been like watching a well-choreographed dance. I only wish that those who pay their taxes for David's education could have witnessed the upbeat, enthusiastic cooperation this team showed today.

8:45 a.m. As I drive to Midway I find I have changed my car radio from my usual classical station to a station with songs, and I am singing.

9:00 a.m. I am doing a classroom orientation for Bobby and his classmates so they can experience and feel comfortable with the FM that Bobby will be using. As I begin talking about it, I tell Bobby to put on the headphones. When he gets them in place he looks at me with his sparkling eyes and beautiful smile. I can tell by his expression that he is hearing words and sounds he has never heard before. A most wonderful "aha!" moment. After half an hour the other first graders go off to recess while Bobby and I spend another 15 minutes together with the FM system. He is delighted and delightful.

11:50 a.m. In David's classroom I begin training Paul, a sophomore who has agreed to be David's peer tutor when David returns on Monday. The kids at David's table are finishing a certificate of initial mastery (CIM) writing assignment, so I just sit and help when needed. At 12:45 they're finally finished, so Paul and I go to a quiet spot in the library and discuss different strategies for helping a deaf student understand concepts and new vocabulary. Paul is a quick study, and I'm feeling comfortable that David will have adequate support when I'm not in class with him.

1:15 p.m. One last school before the weekend begins. Justin is a second grader who has atresia and uses a bone conduction aid. Most of the time he wears it at school, but today he's not wearing it because his head has a sore spot from the headband rubbing on it. After adjusting the headband I send him back to class. I'll call his mom later and discuss how to help him avoid sore spots.

3:00 p.m. In our fifth phone conversation of the week, I hear the news from Ellen. The doctor has agreed that David is suffering from clinical depression, and has started him on medication. Hopefully by Monday the true David will reappear in class—tall, gentle, and ready to get on with life.

3:30 p.m. I drive home through the farmland beyond East County, thinking of my students. Spread out among twelve schools, I sometimes wish I could have them all in one K-12 classroom, so I could spend more time with each of them.

But that's selfish. They need all of us on their respective MDTs, so each of the team members can do what he or she does best. I like the versatility my job demands: K-12 instructional support, consultation to faculty and staff, parental contacts, and even the mechanics of checking recalcitrant hearing aids.

—

Because I follow each of my students for a number of years, I can get close to them and their parents. Closer, perhaps, than regular classroom teachers who usually have so many more students. And that pays off in time of crisis, like David's. I expect he will show up Monday morning. Right now I'm worrying more about Sara, who has far less support at home, and Sherry with the mysterious learning disability. But I guess part of my job is to keep worrying about my kids. My car comes to the top of a hill overlooking the end of the Willamette Valley, where immigrants settled after desperate months on the Oregon Trail. For the first time since Monday, bars of sunlight push across the landscape, and the road ahead looks pretty good.